500 SAT® WORDS AND HOW TO REMEMBER THEM FOREVER!

Written by Charles Gulotta

Illustrated by Trish Dardine

Published by
Mostly Bright Ideas

ISBN: 0-9653263-0-6

Contents

Dedication

This book is dedicated to everyone who's ever gone blank while taking a test, or said "profane" when they meant "profound," or wished they'd studied Latin when they had the chance. But most of all, it's dedicated to those of you who believe you just aren't smart enough to learn. Because you certainly are.

Introduction

The purpose of this book

This book exists because there are a bunch of words you need to know. You'll find five hundred of them on the pages that follow.

If learning vocabulary words doesn't seem like a big thrill, try to see the whole picture. It isn't, I admit, as much fun as a cruise ship stocked with jelly doughnuts. At the same time, it's much better than being pushed off a cliff into a dark, rat-infested swamp. Or having abdominal surgery. Or watching bowling on television.

Now that we have things in perspective, let's get to work. But wait a minute, you're thinking. Five hundred words! That's a big number. How will I ever have time to take care of my basic physical requirements, not to mention maintain contact with my family, if I have to learn five hundred words?

Five hundred may seem like a lot, but it really isn't. You can learn all of these words with very little effort. Your brain is capable of absorbing, understanding, and storing millions of facts and ideas. Just think about how many songs you know, how many famous faces you recognize, how many thoughts and memories and images and sounds and voices you can see and hear in your head. Think about how many different kinds of breakfast cereal you can name. Learning five hundred new words should be easy. And it is.

But wait another minute, you're thinking. These aren't just any five hundred words. These are five hundred hard words. These are five hundred of the words I've been trying to avoid. Well, here's the good news: there are no hard words in this book.

Really, there aren't. There are no hard words on the SAT either.

What makes a word hard or easy? Is it the number of letters? The number of syllables? No, you know many words with ten or more letters. You know many words with five or more syllables. And you'd have no trouble defining those words. At the same time, there are short words, some just three or four letters, that neither you nor I could begin to define or explain.

The words that are hard, truly hard, are the ones that have hard-to-understand meanings. Like "erg," for example, a common physics term. Here's the definition of erg as it appears in *Webster's Third New International Dictionary*: "An absolute cgs unit of work representing the work done by a force of one dyne acting through a displacement of one centimeter in the direction of the force." (Notice, by the way, that erg has three letters, one syllable.)

So what's so special about the five hundred words in this book? A few things. For one, they appear frequently on the SAT and other tests. They also tend to show up in college courses. Depending on what you read and who you hang around with, it's likely they will continue to show up for the rest of your life. These are the words that comprise much of the language of educated adulthood.

Does that make them hard? No. Again, these words are not hard. They're just <u>unfamiliar</u>. And that's certainly no cause for despair because every word you know now was, at one time, unfamiliar. (At some point in your life, "house" was a hard word.) Once you get acquainted with a word, once it becomes familiar, it loses its mystery and its power to confuse or frighten you. Eventually it becomes an old friend, one of the "easy" words.

Here's more good news

Almost without exception, the unfamiliar word turns out to have a simple meaning. Look quickly through this book and notice the meanings of the words. You'll find definitions like "big," "small," "fast," "poor," "greedy," and "quiet." There's just nothing difficult about what these words are trying to say to you.

So what <u>is</u> the difficult part? It's this: when you try to remember what these unfamiliar words mean, you have trouble even though their meanings are simple. Why? Because they're not part of your everyday speech and writing. You don't see these words, you don't hear them, and you don't use them. So you've had no reason to remember them.

Until now, that is.

You're looking at this book, so you must have some purpose for wanting to build your vocabulary. Maybe you're preparing for one of the standardized tests. Maybe you want to improve your grades in English class. Or maybe you're just looking to increase your command of the language. Whatever your goal, I believe this book will help you reach it, and quickly.

How it all works

For each of the five hundred words, we're going to start with the unfamiliar word and its simple meaning, and we're going to create a bridge between them. The bridge will be in the form of a picture. This picture is like the missing piece of a jigsaw puzzle. It fits the word perfectly on one end and the meaning on the other. Set it in place and your path from word to meaning is clear.

Let's take a look at one example: the word "avarice."

"Avarice" means "greed." Let's create a picture that helps you connect them. We'll do that by breaking the word avarice in half: Ava rice. Picture a woman named Ava seated at a table, a mound of rice piled in front of her. Ava has her arms around the rice because she doesn't want anyone else to get any. So <u>Ava</u>, with the <u>rice</u>, is demonstrating <u>greed</u>. Concentrate on this picture for a few seconds, together with the idea of greed, and burn the image into your memory. From now on, whenever you see or hear the word avarice, think of Ava and her rice and remember how greedy she is. It's as simple as that.

In some cases, we'll break the word apart, as we just did with "avarice." In others, we'll use a word or phrase that looks or sounds like the word we're learning (for example, "celerity" looks like "celery"). Occasionally we'll use the more common meaning of a word to learn its secondary definition ("wax" as a verb means to grow larger, so we'll picture a ball of wax getting bigger). Approximately one hundred of the words are illustrated with cartoons.

In all cases, as you'll probably notice, the pictures are unusual, bizarre, and ridiculous. This will help you remember them. For some reason, the stranger the image the easier it is to recall.

Now go to page 17 and find the following entry:

AVARICE (AH-ver-iss) *noun* — **greed**

Looks like: Ava rice

Picture: A woman named Ava seated at a table with her arms around a mound of rice; she won't share the rice with anyone. She's greedy.

Other form: Avaricious *(adj)*

Every one of the five hundred words will appear in this format. The word to be learned is in bold uppercase letters, followed by its pronunciation, part of speech, and definition.

The next line down suggests a cue, based on what the word looks or sounds like. In the example, the cue for "avarice" was "Ava rice." This cue will help you recall the suggested picture, which will immediately lead you to the word's meaning. (If this sounds like too much work, just try a few and you'll see that it isn't. You will remember the cues, pictures, and meanings quickly and on a long-term basis.)

The next line describes a picture or tells a story that illustrates the word and its meaning. A few of these stories are longer than you might expect, but again, you don't have to memorize them. All you need to take away from each entry is the meaning of the word and the image that will help you remember it.

The phrase "Other form" presents the word you're learning as it appears in other parts of speech. So when you learn "avarice" as a noun you'll also learn "avaricious" as an adjective.

With many of the words you'll also find a "Note" at the bottom of the entry. These notes tell you to make a mental connection with other words, or warn you about being confused by a similar-looking word. Sometimes the note will point out the root of the word and suggest other words with the same root. Check out these related words in the dictionary to further build your vocabulary.

Just a quick comment on pronunciation. I've avoided using the dictionary method of explaining how to pronounce a word, mostly because the dictionary uses weird stuff like upside-down "e"s and dots over letters and I find those things confusing. I've spelled out the pronunciations, with the accented syllables in uppercase, based on the way I say the words. I mention this because we're often creating pictures based on what the words <u>sound</u> like. Your pronunciation may be slightly different.

At the end of this book you'll find a list of words that should have been included but weren't, either because there was no more room or because I couldn't think of a picture. They are just as important as the five hundred in the main part of the book, and you should make a point of learning them. Beginning on page 116, you'll also find some helpful hints for approaching the SAT's verbal section. You'll learn about some of the many sources of confusion in the English language -- such as look-alike and sound-alike words -- how the testmakers take advantage of that confusion, and how you can avoid falling into the traps they've set for you on the SAT.

So what now?

That's completely up to you. How much and how quickly do you want to learn? I've used this technique to help students learn as many as thirty words in an hour. However, five at a time seems to be a comfortable number for most people. It might help to write the words down as you learn them, along with short, one or two-word definitions. If some words give you trouble, include a description of the picture for those words. For example: "Avarice -- greed -- Ava and her rice." Then, as you add to your list, look over the words you've already learned. You may find that after reviewing a word two or three times, you no longer need the picture. You'll just come up with the definition, as if you've always known it.

A special note to younger students

You may not be familiar with the SAT yet, but in a few years it will suddenly become very important. If you're already working with this book, you're off to a great start. Keep learning new words wherever and whenever you can. Knowing the meanings of many different words is a skill that will help you a great deal on the SAT -- and for the rest of your life.

Read, read, read!

Remembering the meaning of a word is only the first step. This may sound strange, but try to get acquainted with each word. Learn how to spell it, and how to recognize its other forms. Notice how it's used in books and newspapers. Then, gradually, work the word into your writing and speech. Eventually it will become a natural part of your language. That's when you've truly learned it.

Building a strong vocabulary is a lifelong process. I hope this book helps to make it a little easier, and a little more fun.

ABSTRACT (ab-STRAHKT) *adj* — theoretical; not concrete

Think of: absent tracks

Picture: A steam train riding on invisible tracks. The tracks are abstract, just an idea.

Other form: Abstraction *(noun)*

ABSTRUSE (ab-STROOSE) *adj* — difficult to understand

Sounds like: Abb's truce

Picture: A hillbilly holding a rifle in one hand and a note in the other. The note may be a truce from the family he's been feuding with (the Abbs), but he's not sure because it's hard to understand.

Other forms: Abstrusely *(adv)*; abstruseness *(noun)*

ACCLAIM (uh-CLAME) *verb* — praise; applaud

Sounds like: a claim

Picture: The office of an insurance company. The newcomer on the staff has just handled her first claim. Her co-workers, a supportive bunch, are all clapping for her and offering their congratulations.

Other forms: Acclaim, acclamation *(nouns)*

Note: Don't confuse with "acclimation," which is the process of becoming adjusted to a new situation.

ACCOLADE (AKK-oh-lade) *noun* — an award, or praise

Sounds like: echo lad

Picture: A young lad is standing on the edge of a cliff, facing a vertical wall of rock about a hundred feet away. He yells wonderful things about himself so that his voice echoes off the wall and comes back to him. He listens and smiles as the words of praise settle over him. "Listen to those accolades, you great kid!" he yells. "LISTEN TO THOSE ACCOLADES, YOU GREAT KID!" yells the echo.

ACQUIESCENT (ak-wee-ESS-ent) *adj* — reluctantly agreeable; compliant

Sounds like: agree yes cent

First: Go to COMPLACENT and get that picture in your mind, then come back here.

Picture: The same penny seated on the park bench. The children continue to urge the penny to play with them. Knowing that they will never give up, he eventually gives in and quietly and reluctantly gets up to play with the children. (The cent has agreed, said yes, but in a passive, reluctant way.)

Other forms: Acquiesce *(verb)*; acquiescence *(noun)*

ACRIMONY (AK-rih-mo-nee) *noun* — **words or behavior filled with harshness, anger, or bitterness**

Looks like: acre money

Picture: Two neighboring farmers arguing over who owns a certain acre of land.
Farmer 1: "This is my acre. You want it? Give me my money and it's yours!"
Farmer 2: "Give you your money? This is my land, you big, ugly, stupid farmer. Now get out of here before I say something really acrimonious!"

Other forms: Acrimonious *(adj)*; acrimoniously *(adv)*

ADAMANT (ADD-um-ent) *adj* — **refusing to change; stubborn, unyielding**

Looks like: a dam ant

Picture: A giant ant acting as a dam, blocking a stream. The other ants are upset because they need the water for their colony. "Come on," they say, "get out of the way!" But the large ant refuses to move.

Other form: Adamantly *(adv)*

ADROIT (uh-DROYT) *adj* — **skillful in the use of the hands, or in handling difficult situations**

Looks like: android, which is a human-like robot

Picture: An android playing basketball. He dribbles behind his back and between his legs, and does reverse lay-ups with either hand. The play-by-play commentator is impressed: "He's a wonder to watch. He has the highest level of ability I've ever seen. And he has become equally adroit at handling the media, particularly concerning that whole question of his use of illegal battery packs in the Olympics."

Other forms: Adroitness *(noun)*; adroitly *(adv)*

ADVOCATE (AD-vuh-kate) *verb* — **support; plead for; speak on behalf of**

Sounds like: ad for Kate

Picture: Kate is seeking her first job. She's smart and well-educated, but has no experience, so most people won't even give her an interview. Kate's aunt, publisher of the local newspaper, has always been very supportive of Kate. She begins running ads for Kate in the newspaper. The ads tell the reader how talented and reliable Kate is. "I strongly advocate your hiring her" is the last line of each ad.

Other forms: Advocate, advocacy *(nouns)*

AFFABLE (AFF-uh-bull) *adj* — **friendly; easygoing**

Looks like: a fable

Think of: Aesop's Fables. Picture Aesop, a Greek man who lived about 500 B.C. Imagine him as a very friendly, outgoing person, standing in the center of the village and greeting people as they pass by.

Other forms: Affability *(noun)*; affably *(adv)*

AFFIRMATION (aff-er-MAY-shun) *noun* — **positive statement; assertion; agreement**

Sounds like: a firm Asian

Picture: A muscular man from the Orient being interviewed by a TV news reporter. "We've heard," says the reporter, "that you plan to break the world weightlifting record by lifting a Toyota filled with Sumo wrestlers. Is this true?" "Yes," replies the Asian man. "And that includes a full tank of gas and maps in the glove compartment." Looking into the TV camera, the reporter says, "Up until now it had been just another unfounded rumor. But now we've received affirmation."

Other forms: Affirm *(verb);* affirmative *(adj);* affirmatively *(adv)*

ALIENATE (AIL-ee-uh-nate) *verb* — **to push someone away, or cause him to separate from people**

Sounds like: Alien Nate

Picture: Nate, a Martian, is standing apart from a group of former Earthling friends. One says, "We don't want him around anymore. He's weird. It's like he's from another planet or something."

Other forms: Alien, alienation *(nouns)*

ALOOF (uh-LOOF) *adj* — **detached; apart; indifferent**

Sounds like: a roof

Picture: Person on the roof of a house, refusing to even look at the people below. He has completely removed himself from the group.

ALTRUISTIC (al-troo-ISS-tik) *adj* — **unselfish; caring**

Sounds like: Al True's Wish Stick

Picture: A man named Al True has a "wish stick," or magic wand. He uses it to help people by giving them what they need.

Other form: Altruism *(noun)*

AMBIDEXTROUS (am-bee-DEX-truss) *adj* — **able to use both hands with equal skill**

Sounds like: Bambi Dextrous

Picture: A baseball pitcher named Bambi Dextrous who pitches with both hands at the same time.

Connect with: Dexterity

AMBIGUOUS (am-BIG-yoo-uss) *adj* — **unclear; vague; having several possible interpretations**

Sounds like: a big U.S.

Picture: Mother and son are standing at the front door. Son is about to leave on a trip.
    Mom: So where exactly are you going?
    Son: Somewhere.
    Mom: Somewhere where?
    Son: Somewhere in the U.S.
    Mom: You're being very vague. It's a big U.S. out there.

Other forms: Ambiguity *(noun);* ambiguously *(adv)*

AMBIVALENCE (am-BIV-uh-lence) *noun* — **indecision; feeling of being pulled in two directions**

Looks like: Val inside ambulance (ambiVALence)

Picture: A woman named Val is about to have a baby. She's gone into labor while her husband is at work. She's called for an ambulance to take her to the hospital, but now that she's inside the ambulance she's having second thoughts about going without her husband: "Wait! Let's give him a few more minutes. No, we should go. I'm in labor. Okay, take me to the hospital. No, wait! Maybe he'll get here soon..."

Other forms: Ambivalent *(adj);* ambivalently *(adv)*

AMELIORATE (uh-MEEL-ee-or-ate) *verb* — **to make an unpleasant situation better; to improve**

Sounds like: a meteor ate

Picture: A house was overrun with two-headed snakes. Suddenly, a meteor swooped down and gobbled up all the snakes. So a meteor ate the snakes and improved the situation in the house.

Other form: Amelioration *(noun)*

AMITY (AM-ih-tee) *noun* — **friendship**

Sounds like: Emma tea

Picture: A lady named Emma who invites neighbors and passersby over to her house for tea every day. Visitors are lined up at the front door, while a steady stream of people holding teacups flows from the back door and spills out onto the back lawn. A smiling Emma says, "I'm just trying to be friendly."

Connect with: Amicable *(adj)*, amigo *(Spanish)*

AMORPHOUS (ay-MORF-uss) *adj* — **without form or shape**

Sounds like: "Yay, more for us!"

Picture: A mother bringing her three children bowls of some shapeless food. One of the kids says, "Yay, more for us!" One of the others says, "Yeah, but more what?"

ANALOGOUS (uh-NAHL-uh-guss) *adj* — **similar**

Sounds like: an alligator

Picture: Two alligators that look exactly alike.

Other form: Analogy *(noun)*

ANARCHY (AN-arr-kee) *noun* — **a lack of order; chaos**

Sounds like: an ark key

Picture: The animals on Noah's Ark are running wild. Noah, standing on the pier, has somehow been locked out. He's yelling, "My key! Please, someone give me an ark key! This is chaos!"

Other form: Anarchist *(noun)*

ANATHEMA (uh-NATH-a-ma) *noun* — **a religious curse, or the thing or person being cursed**

Looks like: an anthem

Picture: A man who, many years ago, fled his native country because of the cruel government in power there. Now, as an old man, he finds a record in his attic. When he plays the record, he hears, for the first time in four decades, the national anthem of his former home. The song reminds him of the cruel dictator still in power and he spits on the record, cursing the words, the dictator, and the entire government. The anthem is now anathema to him.

Other form: Anathematize *(verb)*

ANTAGONISTIC (an-tag-uh-NISS-tik) *adj* — **in hostile competition; opposing**

Sounds like: ant tag on his stick

Picture: An ant holding a stick; on the stick hangs a tag that says, "I'll fight anybody, any time. How about right now?"

Other forms: Antagonist, antagonism *(nouns)*; antagonize *(verb)*

ANTIQUATED (ANN-tih-quay-ted) *adj* — **too old to be useful; outdated; obsolete**

Sounds like: Auntie Katie

Picture: A very, very old woman named Auntie Katie. She lives in an old house with an old dog and old furniture. Every single thing in Auntie Katie's life is antiquated.

Connect with: Antique, antiquity *(nouns)*

12

ANTITHESIS (ann-TITH-ih-sis) *noun* — **opposite**

Sounds like: anTEETHesis

Picture: The teeth in your mouth. For every tooth, there is an opposite tooth. For example, for every upper tooth, there is a corresponding (opposite) lower tooth.

Other form: Antithetical *(adj)*

APATHY (APP-uh-thee) *noun* — **lack of interest or concern**

Sounds like: apple tree

Picture: George Washington's father is questioning him about the cherry tree that has been chopped down. Young George, arms folded, replies: "I cannot tell a lie. I really don't <u>care</u> who chopped down the cherry tree."

Other form: Apathetic *(adj)*

APEX (AY-pex) *noun* — **top; highest point; summit**

Looks like: ape x

Picture: King Kong (the ape) climbing the Empire State Building. He's trying to get to a large letter "X" which is perched on top of the building's antenna (the highest point). As he climbs, he thinks to himself, "This will be the apex of my career."

APPEASE (uh-PEEZ) *verb* — **calm; pacify**

Sounds like: peas

Picture: A young child who's upset because he's hungry. He calms down when his mother gives him some peas (this requires a little extra imagination). Or, just think of "please" or "a peace," all of which sound like appease and suggest its meaning.

Other form: Appeasement *(noun)*

ARBITRARY (ARR-bih-treh-ree) *adj* — **selected by random choice and without solid reason**

Sounds like: our bee, Jerry

Picture: A giant glass tank called the Lost Bee Shelter. A young man is looking into the tank at thousands of flying bees. He says to the attendant, "I think that's him. That's our bee, Jerry."

Other form: Arbitrarily *(adv)*

ARCANE (ar-KANE) *adj* — secret; mysterious

Sounds like: our cane

Picture: A child sits at his grandparents' dinner table. In the corner of the room is a wooden cane with mysterious words and markings all over it. When the boy asks what it all means, his grandmother just smiles slightly and says mysteriously, "Oh, that's just our cane. Don't worry about it. You wouldn't understand anyway."

ARCHAIC (arr-KAY-ik) *adj* — old; antiquated

Sounds like: our cake

Picture: A very old cake, covered with cobwebs. One person asks, "Where did we get our cake?" The other person answers, "From Auntie Katie, where else?" (See ANTIQUATED.)

ARROGANT (AHR-oh-gint) *adj* — acting superior, obnoxious, smug, or rude

Looks like: arrow can't

Picture: It's the mid-1800s, somewhere in Oklahoma. A traveling rifle salesman is making a presentation to some Navaho Indians. "You're still using those bows and arrows for hunting?" he asks. "This rifle fires bullets. Do you people know what bullets are?" The Navaho look at each other, annoyed but patient. The salesman continues: "A bullet can take down a buffalo from five hundred yards. An arrow can't! A bullet can fly faster than a hawk. An arrow can't! And a bullet can be kept in your pocket or pouch. An arrow can't! You have to buy my rifles and bullets, because they're better than anything you're using."

Other forms: Arrogance *(noun);* arrogantly *(adv)*

ARTICULATE (ar-TICK-u-let) *adj* — able to speak clearly and effectively

Looks like: Artie Kool-Aid

Picture: A man named Artie holding a pitcher, giving a speech: "...and let me assure you, dear fellows, that it would be a veritable impossibility for me to be so eloquent without this extraordinary thirst-quenching concoction, Kool-Aid."

Other forms: Articulation *(noun)*, articulate *(verb)*

ASCENDANCE (uh-SEN-dence) *noun* — domination; controlling power

Sounds like: a sun dance

Picture: This Indian tribe has been doing rain dances for many centuries. But now it's been raining for seven weeks and they need the sun to dry up the water. So they create and perform a sun dance. After the dancers have been performing for several minutes, the clouds disappear and the sun comes out. The tribe, at least on this occasion, seems to have gained ascendance over the sun.

Other forms: Ascendant *(adj);* ascendancy *(noun)*

ASCETIC (uh-SET-ik) *noun* — **person who rejects physical comfort and luxury for self-discipline.**

Sounds like: acidic (containing a high level of acid)

Picture: A man of great religious faith has decided to leave his comfortable life behind in order to reach a higher level of spiritual growth. He gives away all of his possessions, including his house, donates his savings to charity, and begins to walk across the desert. Many days later, his shoes worn through and his clothes in tatters, he reaches the end of the desert and finds himself at a gas station. A mechanic, recognizing the religious man's obvious need for a drink, offers him a cold can from the vending machine. However, the man sees the soft drink as a luxury, an aspect of the physical world no longer part of his life, and rejects it, choosing instead to drink from a nearby bucket of battery acid. Surprised, the mechanic says, "Why, that's downright acidic!" "I think you mean 'ascetic,'" says the religious man, between sips.

Other forms: Ascetic (adj); asceticism *(noun);* ascetically *(adv)*

ASPERITY (uh-SPERR-ih-tee) *adj* — **roughness; harshness; irritability**

Sounds like: a spirit tea

Picture: A group of ghosts (spirits) meeting for their afternoon tea. One of the spirits gets extremely agitated and angry after drinking his tea, and begins yelling at his companions. (One of the other ghosts comments: "He really needs to start drinking decaffeinated. This regular stuff just haunts him.")

Connect with: Aspersion *(noun)* — a defaming remark

ASSAIL (uh-SAIL) *verb* — **attack with words or force**

Sounds like: a sail (or, a sale)

Picture: The husband comes home with another new sail for the boat. The wife attacks: "What? You spent more money on that stupid boat? You haven't bought yourself a new shirt in six years, but the sailboat is always right in style! What excuse do you have this time?" Husband: "It was on sale."

Other forms: Assailable *(adj);* assailant *(noun)*

ASSIDUOUS (uh-SIJ-yoo-us) *adj* — **persistent; hard-working; diligent; attentive to detail**

Sounds like: a Sid, U.S.

Picture: A devoted worker at the post office has noticed a letter sent from overseas. The envelope is addressed simply, "Sid, U.S." The worker, determined to see that the letter is delivered to the right person, has gathered every telephone directory in the country and is carefully going through each one page-by-page, making a list of every Sid in the U.S. "A Sid, U.S.," he says. "If I'm persistent and pay close attention to detail, I'll find him. Or her."

Other forms: Assiduousness *(noun);* assiduously *(adv)*

ASSUAGE (uh-SWAYJ) *verb* — **relieve; ease; pacify**

Sounds like: as wage

Picture: A fairy godmother appears to a miserable man who is seated at a table piled high with bills. The man is obviously distressed because he has no money. The fairy offers to pay the man a salary ("as wage") for the work he's doing in paying the bills! The man is thrilled, for she has assuaged his anxiety.

Other form: Assuagement *(noun)*

ASTUTE (uh-STOOT) *adj* — **wise; insightfully clever; shrewd**

Sounds like: a stew

Picture: As his students prepare their dishes, the cooking teacher strolls around the kitchen, peeking into each pot and casserole. He's puzzled by the contents of one stove-top pot, but after quickly scanning the ingredients, he looks the young chef straight in the eye and says, "A stew." And of course, he's right.

Other forms: Astutely *(adv)*; astuteness *(noun)*

ATROPHY (AH-troh-phee) *verb* — **waste away; wither**

Looks like: a trophy

Note: The word atrophy usually refers to the way muscles waste away when they haven't been used.

Picture: A trophy with a figure on top. The figure's arms or legs are melting (its muscles have atrophied).

Other form: Atrophy *(noun)*

AUDACIOUS (aw-DAY-shuss) *adj* — **brazen; brash; nervy**

Sounds like: all day shhh's

Picture: A librarian, referring to a boy talking at a nearby table: "'Shhhh,' I say, 'please Shhhh,' all day 'Shhhh's' and he just keeps talking. What brashness! What nerve! What audacity!" The boy turns to the librarian and says, "Shhhh! I'm trying to read!"

Other forms: Audacity *(noun)*; audaciously *(adv)*

AUGMENT (awg-MENT) *verb* — **make larger; increase**

Looks like: Aug. mint

Picture: The gardener has been trying to grow mint for months, with just a few plants to show for her hard work. Then, on August 1st, she discovers her entire backyard covered with mint. "Wow!" she says. "This Aug. mint is quite an increase from the July mint!"

Other form: Augmentation *(noun)*

AUSPICIOUS (aw-SPIH-shuss) *adj* — taking place under promising conditions; likely to succeed

Sounds like: our space shoes

Picture: Two astronauts have just landed on the planet Neptune. Looking out the window of their space-ship, they see that they are surrounded by a frozen lake. In order to accomplish their mission, they must cross the ice and return to the spaceship quickly. One astronaut thinks it's going to be very difficult. The other pulls out two pairs of special boots fitted with large ice skate blades. "This will be easy," he says. Then, gesturing to the boots, "Our space shoes!"

Other forms: Auspiciousness *(noun);* auspiciously *(adv)*

AUSTERE (aw-STEER) *adj* — stern; plain; without luxuries

Sounds like: our steer

Picture: A rancher giving a tour of his ranch: "And this is our steer. He lives in this simple barn, eats plain dry grass, and frowns a lot. We're not sure why."

Other forms: Austerity *(noun);* austerely *(adv)*

AVARICE (AH-ver-iss) *noun* — greed

Looks like: Ava rice

Picture: A woman named Ava seated at a table, her arms around a mound of rice. She won't share the rice with anyone. She's greedy.

Other form: Avaricious *(adj)*

AVERSE (uh-VERSE) *adj* — feeling repelled; wanting to avoid

Looks exactly like: a verse

Picture: A young boy running from the classroom, screaming "Poetry! I can't listen to poetry! Not even a averse!" (Averse sounds a little like reverse, so also think of a person going in reverse to avoid something.)

Note: Don't confuse with "adverse," which means unfavorable. Strong rains may produce <u>adverse</u> conditions for golf. A golfer may be <u>averse</u> to playing in the rain.

BALEFUL (BAIL-full) *adj* — harmful; menacing

Sounds like: bale fall

Picture: Gigantic, heavy bales of hay falling from the sky. One of the bales is about to fall onto someone.

Other form: Balefully *(adv)*

BANAL (ba-NAHL) *adj* — **boring; trite; insipid**

Looks like: ban Al

Picture: A club's members want to keep Al from joining. "I say we ban Al," says one. "He's too boring."

Other form: Banality *(noun)*

BEGUILE (be-GYLE) *verb* — **to cheat or deceive, usually through charm; also, to amuse**

Sounds a little like: beg a while

Picture: Two children plotting to talk their parents into something. The older child says to the younger, "Let's try this. You go out there and beg a while. They love when you do that. They think it's cute. They'll laugh, they'll say, 'Come here and give us a hug, you cute thing,' and then they'll say yes."

Other forms: Beguiling *(adj)*; beguilingly *(adv)*

Connect with: Guile, which means deceitful shrewdness.

BELIE (be-LIE) *verb* — **to give an impression that is the opposite of the way things really are; to misrepresent**

Looks like: bee lie

Picture: A scientist is studying the daily routines of a bumble bee, keeping careful records of what the bee does and when. Like all bees, this one is energetic and hard-working, but also like other bees, this one enjoys a good practical joke. Every day at one o'clock in the afternoon, the bee lies down on a tiny toy couch in the scientist's office and pretends to watch "All My Children." The scientist, of course, is

 surprised by the bee's behavior and notes it every day in his journal: "Every day at one, the bee lies down on the couch and watches television. Where is the industrious busy bee we've all heard about?"

BELLIGERENT (buh-LIJ-er-int) *adj* — **having a strong tendency to argue and fight**

Sounds like: bell ledger rent

Picture: The landlord is standing at your door, holding his rent ledger and ringing a large bell. By the time you open the door to see what's going on, he's rung the bell three or four more times. "Where's your rent?" he asks angrily, waving his ledger in the air. "It was due an hour ago. I'm going to stand right here and ring this bell and wave this ledger until I have your rent. And if you don't like it, you can just step outside and I'll punch you so hard you won't remember to say ouch. Come on out here, you miserable cheating lowlife deadbeat!"

Other forms: Belligerence *(noun)*; belligerently *(adv)*

Note: The root "belli" has to do with fighting or war. Connect this word with "bellicose," which has almost the same meaning.

BENEDICTION (ben-neh-DIK-shun) *noun* — **good wishes; a blessing**

Sounds like: Benedict shine

Picture: Benedict, who always says good and encouraging things to people, so that they come away from him shining with happiness.

Note: Any word beginning with the prefix "bene-" has a positive meaning, and usually refers to a good result (or benefit).

BENEVOLENT (beh-NEV-oh-lent) *adj* — **kindhearted; good-natured; generous**

Sounds like: Ben Elephant

Picture: A kindly old elephant named Ben who lives at the zoo. He saves the peanuts that visitors give him and takes them to the other animals late at night. "That Ben Elephant," says one bear to another, "what a nice guy!"

Other forms: Benevolence *(noun);* benevolently *(adv)*

BENIGN (beh-NINE) *adj* — **gentle; kind-hearted; mild**

Sounds like: be nine

Picture: A machine that measures a person's kindness level. Its meter ranges from 1 to 9, with 9 designated as "extremely kind and gentle." A girl places the electrode helmet on her head, pulls the lever, and prays, "Oh, I hope I'm a nine! Be nine! Please be nine!"

Other form: Benignly *(adv)*

BEQUEATH (be-KWEETH) *verb* — **to leave behind or hand down through a will; transmit**

Rhymes with: beneath

Picture: The reading of a will. "...And to my son, Robert, who always thought my possessions were beneath him, I bequeath something that is beneath him: the rug on the floor in this room."

Other forms: Bequeathal, bequest *(nouns)*

BLIGHT (BLITE) *noun* — **decay; disease; widespread death**

Looks like: B light

Picture: An entire orchard of fruit trees has died. A scientist hired to study the situation concludes: "The problem is too much B-light. B-light is that part of the light spectrum emitted by car headlights. These trees were too close to the road, and the headlights wiped them out."

Other forms: Blight *(verb);* blighted *(adj)*

BOLSTER (BOLE-ster) *verb* — **to support; to reinforce**

Sounds like: bowl stir

Picture: A mixing bowl, filled with cake batter, is talking to the wooden spoon: "Come on spoon, stir that batter. I know you can do it!" (The batter joins in: "Hey, you're really bolstering the spoon's confidence! This cake may just pan out after all!")

BOMBAST (BOMM-bast) *noun* — **speech or writing intended to impress the audience; pompous**

Sounds like: bomb blast

Picture: A convention of scientists who specialize in explosives. The speaker is talking about his latest discovery: "Ladies and gentlemen, without bragging I must tell you that this invention will change the world. My bomb fits in the palm of the hand, yet one such device produces a blast that can destroy all of North America and rattle teacups in London. It is, probably, the greatest single advance in the history of mankind, if I may say so..."

Other form: Bombastic *(adj)*

BREVITY (BREV-uh-tee) *noun* — **briefness; conciseness**

Sounds like: Bravo Tea

Picture: Tea that takes just a few seconds to make. Also, when people drink Bravo Tea, they say what they have to say in very few words. It gives them the gift of brevity.

BUMPTIOUS (BUMP-shuss) *adj* — **pushy; obnoxiously self-assertive**

Sounds like: bump chess

Picture: A man and woman are playing chess. The man is annoying, pushy, and rude. Whenever he captures one of his opponent's pieces, he bumps it off the board and yells out, "Bump chess! I love this game! And I really love winning!"

Other forms: Bumptiousness *(noun);* bumptiously *(adv)*

CACOPHONY (kuh-KAH-fuh-nee) *noun* — **a collection of sounds or voices that don't blend well; harshness of sound**

Looks like: a combination of "cocoon" and "symphony"

Picture: A cocoon hanging from the branch of a tree. Inside, a caterpillar on his way to becoming a butterfly has decided to make good use of the time by learning to play the violin. On this particular day, the caterpillar is playing an entire symphony, although not very well. Outside, birds and squirrels are covering their ears, trying to escape the cacophony coming from the cocoon.

Other forms: Cacophonous *(adj);* cacophonously *(adv)*

Note: The root "phone" has to do with sound, as in "telephone."

CAJOLE (cuh-JOLE) *verb* — **to fool with flattery or false promises; coax; deceive**

Sounds like: cage hole

Picture: A large cat sits outside a parakeet's cage. The cage has a small hole at the top. Inside, a parakeet is perched on a swing. "You have the most beautiful feathers I've ever seen," says the cat. "The colors are magnificent. Why don't you squeeze out through that hole so I can get a better look at you?"

Other forms: Cajolery, cajolement *(nouns)*

MISS DOOR, LET ME BE CANDID... YOUR KNEES ARE KNOBBY, YOU BECOME UNHINGED WHEN THE TEMPO CHANGES, AND YOU NEVER SEEM TO KNOW IF YOU'RE OPENING OR CLOSING. I'M NOT KNOCKING YOU, BUT DON'T RING OUR BELL, WE'LL RING YOURS.

CANDOR (CANNED-er) *noun* — **honesty; frankness**

Looks like: can door

Picture: A door on stage. The door is trying out for a dance job. The producer, a tin can, is delivering the bad news with as much honesty as possible.

Other forms: Candid *(adj)*; candidly *(adv)*

CAPACIOUS (cuh-PAY-shuss) *adj* — **large; roomy; spacious**

Sounds like: car patients

Picture: A doctor who uses a car as her office. As she explains, "This car has an incredible amount of room inside. The front seat is a waiting area and the back seat has three separate examining rooms."

Other forms: Capaciousness *(noun)*; capaciously *(adv)*

CAPITULATE (kuh-PITCH-oo-late) *verb* — **surrender; yield**

Looks like: capital late

Picture: The government of a small nation has just been overthrown by a neighboring country. In the capital city of the overthrown nation, the president is speaking with his military commander, who has just arrived with troops. "I'm sorry," he says, "but you got here too late. I was forced to surrender."

Other form: Capitulation *(noun)*

CAPRICIOUS (cuh-PREE-shuss) *adj* — **unpredictable**

Looks like: cap riches

Picture: A man standing in front of a slot machine in a casino. He puts a quarter into the slot, pulls the handle, and holds his cap under the chute, waiting hopefully for his riches. He doesn't know if or when it will happen, but he's sure it <u>could</u> happen.

Other forms: Capriciously *(adv)*; caprice *(noun)*

21

CASTIGATE (CASS-tig-ate) *verb* — **scold; punish**

Sounds like: curse the gate

Picture: Someone scolding a gate.

Synonyms: Admonish, berate, censure, chasten, chastise, denounce, disparage, objurgate, rebuke, reprimand, reprove, upbraid...

CAUSTIC (CAWSE-tik) *adj* — **burning, either with chemicals or sarcasm**

Sounds like: caw stick

Picture: A crow crying ("caw, caw") because it has been burned by a stick coated with acid.

CELERITY (seh-LEHR-ih-tee) *noun* — **speed**

Looks like: celery

Picture: A stalk of celery moving at high speed. The celery might be in the form of a race car zooming around the track.

Connect with: Accelerate.

CENSURE (SEN-shur) *verb* — **to criticize**

Sounds like: send ashore

Picture: A man wading to shore from a large sailing ship. He is the navigator of the ship, and has been sent ashore by the captain and the rest of the crew because they blame him for getting them lost at sea. They have sent him to ask directions from the people on the beach. As he walks, they shout at him from the ship: "You couldn't find your way across a bathtub!" "Try not to miss the beach!"

Other forms: Censorious *(adj);* censoriously *(adv)*

Note: Don't confuse with "censor," which means "to delete objectionable material."

CHASTEN (CHAY-sen) *verb* — **punish; discipline; castigate**

Sounds like: chase sin

Picture: An old-fashioned, religious mother who is trying to discipline her mischievous son: "I'll keep scolding and punishing until I've chased the sin right out of you!"

Connect with: Chastise

Note: Don't confuse with "chaste," which means "pure."

CHASTISE (CHASS-tize) *verb* — **scold; punish; castigate**

Sounds like: chase ties

Picture: The same man who yelled at the gate (see CASTIGATE) is now chasing ties around the yard, scolding them.

Other form: Chastisement *(noun)*

CHOLER (KAH-ler) *noun* — **anger**

Sounds like: collar

Picture: A dog who's very angry about the ridiculous collar he's been forced to wear.

Other form: Choleric *(adj)*

CIRCUMSCRIBE (SIR-kum-skribe) *verb* — **draw a line around; define limits; confine; restrict**

Looks like: circus crib

Picture: The baby elephant is headed for a career in the circus, but she has a lot to learn. Her trainer puts the elephant in a baby crib and places the crib inside one of the circus rings. The elephant may climb out of the crib, but may not go outside the circle, her limit. Her movements have been circumscribed.

Other forms: Circumscribable *(adj);* circumscription *(noun)*

Note: The prefix "circum" means "around." Think about the following words, and look up the ones you don't know: circumcise, circumference, circumlocution, circumnavigate, circumspect, circumvent.

CIRCUMSPECT (SIR-kum-spekt) *adj* — **cautious**

Sounds like: search inspect

Picture: The chipmunk peeks out from her home — a hole in the trunk of a hollow tree. She must go out for food, but before leaving the safety of her tree, she carefully and methodically looks around (searches and inspects) to see if a predator is waiting to snatch her.

Other forms: Circumspectly *(adv);* circumspection *(noun)*

CLEMENCY (KLEM-en-see) *noun* — **mercy**

Sounds like: clam in sea

Picture: A clam as judge presiding over an undersea courtroom. The defendant is a mussel accused of fixing races at the snail track. Judge: "The maximum sentence for this crime is one weekend on a dry beach filled with small children and biology teachers. But it's your first offense, so I'll show clemency. I hereby sentence you to eight hours of voluntary service working with oil spill survivors."

Other form: Clement *(adj)*

OK, PRIVACY CAN BE REALLY NICE, BUT PEARL, IT'S BEEN 9 YEARS!

KNOCK KNOCK

CLOISTER (CLOY-ster) *noun* — **secluded or isolated from the outside world; also, a place of seclusion**

Sounds like: closed oyster

Picture: A giant closed oyster. Someone is hiding inside the shell.

COALESCE (KO-uh-less) *verb* — **unite; grow together**

Sounds like : coal S

Picture: A man puts some charcoal into his barbecue grill, throws in a match, and goes into the house. When he returns, he sees that the coals have come together to form a large letter "S" at the bottom of the grill. "When they say it makes a Super Fire, they aren't kidding!"

Other forms: Coalescent *(adj);* coalescence *(noun)*

COERCE (ko-ERSE) *verb* — **to force someone by threatening or physically overpowering him**

Sounds like: course

Picture: A young Army private has to run an obstacle course, which requires him to climb a flaming wall, swim across a pond filled with hungry alligators, and run through a field of rattlesnakes. The soldier is reluctant to run the course, but his sergeant forces him with threats of physical harm, verbal abuse, isolation, double shifts in the mess hall, and courtmartial.

Other forms: Coercion *(noun);* coercive *(adj);* coercively *(adv)*

COMPLACENT (kum-PLAY-sent) *adj* — **self-satisfied; unconcerned**

Sounds like: come play, cent

Picture: A penny sits on a park bench. Two small children call to him, "Come play, Cent!" But the penny, smiling, hands behind head, eyes closed, is too self-satisfied to move from the bench.

Other forms: Complacence, complacency *(nouns)*

COMPLIANT (kum-PLY-ent) *adj* — **to change your behavior at someone else's request; conforming; obeying; yielding**

Looks almost exactly like: complaint

Picture: The man working in the complaint department of a store has put up a sign over his desk that says, "COMPLAINT." His boss has walked by nine or ten times, and each time has told the man to change the spelling to "COMPLIANT." Even though he knows it's incorrect, the employee gives in and makes the change. So now he works directly under a sign that says, "COMPLIANT."

Other forms: Compliance *(noun);* comply *(verb)*

COMPOSURE (kum-POE-zher) *noun* — **calmness; equanimity**

Sounds like: Camp Pozer

Picture: A summer camp, called Camp Pozer, where the counselors and campers lie down all day long. Everyone is always calm and relaxed. Awards are given out for the longest naps.

Other form: Compose *(verb)*

CONCEDE (kun-SEED) *verb* — **admit reluctantly; yield**

Sounds like: corn seed

Picture: Two farmers. One, examining something under a magnifying glass, admits that it *is* corn seed.

Other form: Concession *(noun)*

Note: A concession speech is one in which the loser of an election reluctantly admits that his or her opponent has won.

CONCISE (kun-SISE) *adj* — **short and to the point; terse**

Sounds like: Kahn's Ice

Picture: A company, called "Kahn's Ice," that sells and delivers blocks of ice. The slogan on their truck is "Cold."

Other forms: Conciseness *(noun);* concisely *(adv)*

CONCUR (kun-KERR) *verb* — **agree**

Sounds like: can curl

Picture: Two hairstylists discussing a customer's hair. "I believe it can curl," says one. The other concurs, or agrees.

Other form: Concurrence *(noun)*

CONDONE (kun-DONE) *verb* — **to overlook, excuse, or pardon**

Looks like: condo one

Picture: The owner of a condominium complex is showing her brother around. At condo one, he notices that the tenants have covered the outside of the building with multi-colored aluminum siding, placed a huge neon sign that flashes "We're number 1!" in the living room window, and trimmed the shrubs to look like characters from "Gilligan's Island." When he asks why she would condone these changes, she replies, "They pay their rent."

Note: Don't confuse with "condemn," which means "to criticize."

CONFOUND (kon-FOUND) *verb* — **to mix up (in your own mind); or, to confuse someone else**

Sounds like: gun found

Picture: A detective investigating a murder. The victim was found in a windowless room, the door locked from the inside. The murder weapon, a gun, is found inside a locked cabinet, along with the keys to both the door and the cabinet itself. "I'm confounded," admits the detective. "How did this happen?"

Other forms: Confounded *(adj)*; confoundedly *(adv)*

CONSONANCE (KON-so-nence) *noun* — **a blending of sounds or opinions; harmony; agreement**

Sounds exactly like: consonants

Picture: Three consonants from the alphabet — C, K, and Q — are having lunch together. "As far as I'm concerned," says C, "we're in complete agreement. We're all making the same sounds."

Other form: Consonant *(adj)*

CONSUMMATE (KON-soo-mate) *verb* — **to complete or make whole**

Looks like: consume mate

Picture: Black widow spiders have a bizarre end to their mating ritual. After mating is complete, the female actually consumes (eats) the male. Imagine that the male and female come to this horrible agreement beforehand and they both sign a contract stating that the female will have the male for dinner right after they finish mating. They shake (consummating the deal) and have sex (consummating the mating ritual). Then the female consumes her mate (consummating this really disgusting law of nature).

Other forms: Consummation *(noun)*; consummate *(adj)*   Note: As an adjective, "consummate" (KON-soo-met) means "perfect" or "highly-skilled."

CONTEND (kun-TEND) *verb* — **to argue a point or position; or, to struggle for**

Sounds like: can't end

Picture: A football team, losing 118 to 0. In the locker room at halftime, the captain speaks up: "We've fought back all year and it <u>can't end</u> here. If we're to be <u>contenders</u>, we can't give up!"

Other forms: Contention *(noun)*; contentious *(adj)*

CONTINGENT (kun-TIN-jent) *adj* — **dependent upon other circumstances; conditional**

Sounds like: can tin gent

Picture: A man made of tin cans. A friend asks if he's planning to play in the golf tournament next weekend. "It depends," says the can tin gent. "If it's sunny, I'll be there. If it rains, I definitely won't. I haven't played in ten years, so I'm rusty enough already."

Other forms: Contingency *(noun)*; contingently *(adv)*

CONTRACT (kun-TRAKT) *verb* — **squeeze together; shrink**

Looks exactly like: contract (KON-trakt) — a legal document

Picture: Two businesspeople are making a deal of some kind. After they each sign the contract, the document begins to shrink, as if the paper it's written on is being compressed. Says one of the signers, "I thought this deal was going to allow me to expand, but it appears as though it will be just the opposite."

Other forms: Contraction *(noun);* contractible *(adj)*

CONTRITE (kun-TRITE) *adj* — **sorry; penitent**

Sounds like: canned trout

Picture: A large, overfed cat has been discovered in the pantry after he's opened and devoured twelve cans of trout. As his owner hovers angrily over him, the cat appears to be sorry; his face and body seem to be saying, "I promise, I'll never do this again." (The dog of the house watches from a corner of the room and thinks, "I wonder if the cat would teach me how to use that can opener.")

Other form: Contrition *(noun)*

CONUNDRUM (kah-NUN-drum) *noun* — **riddle; mystery**

Looks like: cone and drum

Picture: A man playing the drum, but instead of drumsticks, he's using ice cream cones. An observer asks: "How does he play music with those things?" A second observer: "It's a mystery to me."

CONVERGE (kun-VERJ) *verb* — **move together to meet at a common point**

Sounds like: can merge

Picture: Two separate highways have been re-routed so that the cars <u>can merge</u> into one flow of traffic. These roads now converge.

Other forms: Convergence *(noun);* convergent *(adj)*

CONVICTION (kun-VIK-shun) *noun* — **an opinion that is strongly held**

Sounds like: convict Shawn

Picture: You're part of a jury working on the trial of a man named Shawn. The prosecutor is addressing his opening remarks to the jury: "I believe with all my heart that Shawn is guilty. I <u>know</u> he committed this terrible crime. When you see the evidence, you'll also be sure. And you will convict Shawn."

Other form: Convicted *(adj)*

CONVIVIAL (kun-VIV-ee-yul) *adj* — **fond of parties; sociable**

Looks like: can Vivian
Sounds (a little) like: carnival

Picture: The director from CANDOR. His sister Vivian (also a can) has just opened her own carnival. Can Vivian is the perfect host, because she's so festive and outgoing. She greets every guest at the front gate and introduces them to other visitors.

Other forms: Conviviality *(noun);* convivially *(adv)*

COPIOUS (KO-pee-us) *adj* — **in large quantity; abundant**

Sounds like: copy us

Picture: A classroom with three teachers at the blackboard. Each is filling his or her board with notes. One says to the students, "Copy us. You'll have copious notes by the end of this course!"

Other form: Copiousness *(noun)*

Connect with: Cornucopia

CORDIAL (KOR-jil) *adj* — **friendly; welcoming; gracious**

Sounds like: cord Jill

Picture: A girl named Jill who stands at the post office and hands out cord to customers in case they need to tie up packages. She is known to everyone as the warmest, friendliest person in town.

Other forms: Cordiality *(noun);* cordially *(adv)*

CORPOREAL (kor-POR-ee-ul) *adj* — **having to do with the body or the physical world**

Looks like: corporal

Picture: An Army corporal has become known on the base for his addiction to physical fitness. He is constantly doing push-ups and sit-ups, jogging, or lifting weights. When asked why he spends so much time exercising, the corporal explains that "the body is the most important part of a person and it must be kept in perfect condition." When the corporal is invited by friends to attend a religious ceremony, he responds, "Sorry, but I have no interest in the spirit or the soul or any of those religious ideas. Just the body. I'm going to lift weights all day today."

Other forms: Corporealness *(noun);* corporeally *(adv)*

Connect with: Corporation (a body of people), corpse (a dead body), and corpulent (having a large, overweight body)

CORROBORATE (ker-OBB-er-ate) *verb* — **support with evidence; tell the same story; confirm**

Sounds like: co-robber eight

Picture: Eight people have been arrested and brought to trial for the same robbery. One by one, each of the eight "co-robbers" testifies on the witness stand, carefully answering the prosecutor's questions in exactly the same way the previous person did. So each corroborates the testimony of the others.

Other forms: Corroboration *(noun)*; corroborative *(adj)*

Note: This word is usually used to describe courtroom testimony or evidence. Don't confuse it with "collaborate," which means "to work together" (co-labor).

CRITERIA (cry-TEER-ee-uh) *noun* — **requirements or standards used to make a decision**

Sounds like: cry tearier

Picture: The director is advising an actress who is trying out for a role in the show: "When you get to the part where you find out your horse has died, you must cry tearier. We're using this scene to make our decision about who gets the part, and the more tears, the better your chances."

Other form: Criterion *(singular)*

CRYPTIC (KRIP-tik) *adj* — **hidden; secret; mysterious**

Sounds like: crypt tack

Think of: The word crypt means tomb or underground vault. Imagine someone looking around above ground for a tack, but she can't find it because it's buried in the crypt. Also, she holds a piece of paper with a mysterious message: "Don't bother looking for the tack — it's below you." "Hmmm," she thinks, "that's a pretty cryptic message."

CULPABLE (CULP-uh-bull) *adj* — **guilty; blameworthy**

Sounds like: gulpable

Picture: A little boy has just done something wrong and is being questioned by his mother. He swallows hard, making a "gulp" sound.

Other forms: Culpability *(noun)*; culpably *(adv)*

Connect with: Culprit

CUPIDITY (cue-PID-ih-tee) *noun* — **greed, especially for money**

Looks like: cupid

Picture: Cupid using his bow and arrow to hold up a bank.

29

CURSORY (KERR-sir-ee) *adj* — **quickly and incompletely done; superficial**

Looks like: curse sorry

Picture: A witch who'd changed a woman's husband into a cocker spaniel. Touched by the grieving wife's woeful pleas, the witch admits feeling sorry about inflicting the curse, and agrees to change the husband back into a man. But in her haste she doesn't notice that she's only done half the job: he's still half dog.

DAUNTED (DAWN-ted) *adj* — **dismayed; disheartened; discouraged (made less courageous)**

Sounds like: dawn Ted

Picture: Ted is trying to cross the desert. When he awakens at dawn and looks around, he realizes he'd been walking in circles all night. Now he's about to give up his effort. "I was undaunted," Ted says to himself, "and then came the dawn."

Other forms: Daunt *(verb)*; dauntless *(adj)*; dauntlessly *(adv)*

DECADENCE (DEK-uh-dents) *noun* — **moral decay or decline**

Sounds like: deck of dance

Picture: Two very conservative ladies aboard a cruise ship. They're discussing what goes on down on the dance deck. "It's disgusting," says one. "They get drunk and they dance all night..." "They're animals," says the other. "That's all I can say. They're morally-corrupt, filthy, and decadent."

Other forms: Decadent *(adj)*; decadently *(adv)*

DEFAME (de-FAME) *verb* — **to say things harmful to a person's reputation; malign; vilify**

Sounds like: the frame

Think of: A very valuable picture frame that had been stored at a fine art museum. When the frame disappears, the guilty museum curator tells everyone the cleaning lady stole it, and that she's been stealing from the museum for years. He is defaming her.

Other forms: Defamation *(noun)*; defamatory *(adj)*

DEFERENCE (DEFF-er-ense) *noun* — **the act of yielding to someone else out of respect**

Sounds like: deafer ants

Picture: A family of ants arriving at a music hall. All the ants in this family have trouble with their hearing, but the grandparents are nearly deaf. The younger members of the family, acknowledging that the grandparents are deafer, allow them to sit in the front, closest to the musicians. They're showing deference to their elders.

Other forms: Defer *(verb)*; deferential *(adj)*

DENOUNCE (dee-NOWNCE) *verb* — **criticize; condemn**

Sounds like: dean ounce

Picture: A short, thin college dean, named Dean Ounce, who criticizes everything and everyone at his school. He yells at students: "You're all lazy and dumb and a disgrace to this institution." One of the students says to another, "Pound-for-pound, Dean Ounce is the most critical dean we've ever had."

Other form: Denunciation *(noun)*

DEPLETED (dee-PLEET-id) *verb* — **emptied; drained; used up**

Sounds like: the pleated

Picture: Saleswoman to a customer who is looking through a rack of pants. "I'm sorry," she says, "the pleated ones are all gone."

Other form: Depletion *(noun);* depletable *(adj)*

DEPLORE (dee-PLOR) *verb* — **to express regret or disapproval; complain; criticize**

Sounds like: deep lure

Picture: Two fish in the ocean, discussing a fisherman's baited hook. First fish: "This is disgusting. We're five hundred feet down and we have to look at plastic worms? Why would anyone use such deep lures, anyway?" Second fish: "I guess they're just not interested in those shallow fish that live upstairs."

Other form: Deplorable *(adj)*

DEPRECATE (DEPP-rah-kate) *verb* — **disapprove; belittle**

Sounds like: Debra Kate

Picture: Debra Kate, Dean Ounce's sister (see DENOUNCE). Debra Kate is the headmistress at a girls' boarding school. She is very strict and old-fashioned. Like her brother, she believes her role is to express disapproval, and she constantly lets her students know how unhappy she is with them.

Other form: Deprecatory *(adj)*

Note: Don't confuse this word with "depreciate," which has to do with lowering the value of something.

DERIDE (dee-RIDE) *verb* — **make fun of; ridicule**

Sounds like: the ride

Picture: An amusement park. Two men are laughing uncontrollably at their friend who has just gotten off "The Ride," a roller coaster that obviously frightened the man a great deal. One of them says, "Maybe you'd better stick with the kiddie rides!"

Other form: Derision *(noun)*

DESPONDENT (dih-SPON-dent) *adj*
— feeling hopeless or depressed

Sounds like: the spoon dent

Picture: A man with a very large collection of antique spoons. He sits holding a dented spoon in one hand, his face buried in the other as he cries to his wife.

Other forms: Despondency *(noun)*; despondently *(adv)*

DESPOT (DESS-pot) *noun* — **tyrant**

Looks like: desk pot

Picture: A pot standing on top of a desk, proclaiming to be in complete power: "O.K. I'm in charge here!"

Other forms: Despotism *(noun)*; despotic *(adj)*

DESTITUTE (DESS-tih-toot) *adj* — **poor; lacking possessions**

Sounds like: dusty tooth

Picture: A man so poor that he has only one tooth left (he can't afford dental care). And even that one tooth is dusty, because he doesn't own a toothbrush.

Other form: Destitution *(noun)*

DESULTORY (DESS-ul-tor-ee) *adj* — **lacking a plan; aimless**

Sounds like: this dull story

Picture: The father of the groom has gone up to the microphone to toast the newlyweds. As he begins to speak, the groom says, "Oh no, not this dull story! He just rambles on and on. He doesn't even think about what he wants to say until he gets up there!" (The father begins: "Ladies and gentlemen. Friends and family. Guests. Waiters and waitresses. Thank you for sharing this special day with us. You know, when my son was eleven, some things happened. I don't necessarily know what they are, or even think they have much to do with this very special day. And now that he has taken a bride, I often wonder..."

Other forms: Desultorily *(adv)*; desultoriness *(noun)*

DEXTERITY (dex-TERR-ih-tee) *noun* — **high level of skill, especially with the hands; adroitness**

Sounds like: Decks Terry

Picture: A magician named Terry who is so skillful with a deck of cards that he's known as "Decks Terry." (Some say he can shuffle a deck of cards while they're still in the box.)

Other form: Dexterous *(adj)*   Connect with: Ambidextrous

DIATRIBE (DIE-a-tribe) *noun* — **a bitterly critical speech**

Sounds like: dye a tribe

Picture: The Indian chief is enraged, screaming at a man who has dyed the entire tribe green.

DIGRESS (dye-GRESS) *verb* — **to move away from the main topic when writing or speaking; to go off on a tangent**

Sounds like: die grass

Picture: The guest speaker at the American Lawn Club's annual convention. The speaker's topic is "How to Bring Dead Grass Back to Life." Just a few minutes into his talk, while discussing the problem of dead grass under the barbecue grill, the lecturer begins to tell his audience about a really fun cookout he went to when he was visiting his sister in Arkansas, and the great recipe she gave him for shish kebab, and how his brother-in-law, Mark, cheated at Monopoly, and...

Other form: Digression *(noun)*; digressive *(adj)*; digressively *(adv)*

DILATORY (DILL-uh-torr-ee) *adj* — **causing lateness; stalling**

Looks like: delay story

Picture: A little girl who doesn't want to go to the dentist. She starts to tell her mother a long story about her day at school. Her mother says, "This is just a 'delay story' because you want us to be late."

Other form: Dilatorily *(adv)*   Note: You can almost see the words "delay" and "late" in the word.

DISCERNING (dih-SURR-ning) *adj* — **insightful; perceptive**

Sounds like: this urn Ning

Picture: Two archeologists digging at a site in China. They uncover a vase, or urn, and one of the archeologists begins to describe it after a very brief examination: "This urn? Ning. That is, it's from the Ning Dynasty. It's easy to tell. See this pattern of dragon's teeth along the bottom? That's distinctive of Ning. Also, the color and shape of the handles are clues that this urn is from the Ning Dynasty." The second archeologist adds, "Also, it says right here on the bottom, 'Made during the Ming Dynasty.'"

Other forms: Discern *(verb)*; discernible *(adj)*

DISCLOSE (diss-KLOZE) *verb* — **provide information; reveal**

Sounds like: this close

Picture: Two corporate chairmen are in a meeting. A vice president of one of the companies comes out of the meeting to talk secretly with waiting reporters. Holding two fingers a quarter-inch apart, he whispers, "They're this close to making the deal." Then he says, "But you didn't hear that from me."

Other form: Disclosure *(noun)*

33

DISCORD (DISS-kord) *noun* — **disagreement; dissonance**

Sounds like: this chord

Picture: Four people listening to music and trying to decide what a certain chord is. They all have different opinions. "This chord is C," says one. "No, it isn't," says another, "this chord is F..."

Other forms: Discordant *(adj);* discordantly *(adv)*

DISCOURSE (DISS-korse) *noun* — **exchange of ideas; conversation**

Sounds like: this course

Picture: A college professor, on the first day of class, explaining to her students what the course will be about. "This course is called, 'On the Nature of Talk.' We will explore the history of conversation. We will study videotapes of people talking. We will discuss the fine art of discussion. All tests will, of course, be oral. And I will insist on plenty of talking in class, because this course is about discourse."

Other form: Discourse *(verb)*

DISDAIN (diss-DANE) *noun* — **a feeling of scorn or contempt**

Sounds like: this stain

Picture: Person who refuses to help others remove a stain (he's above that sort of work).

Other forms: Disdain *(verb);* disdainful *(adj)*

DISPARAGE (dis-PAHR-ij) *verb* — **say negative things; belittle**

Sounds like: this asparagus

Picture: Two vegetable farmers stand along a fence looking over to the other side, where a third farmer is loading his asparagus crop onto a truck. They are ridiculing him for the small asparagus he's grown. "Asparagus?" asks one. "I thought it was string beans!"

Other forms: Disparaging *(adj);* disparagingly *(adv)*

Note: Don't confuse "disparage" with "disparate."

DISPARATE (dis-PAHR-et) *adj* — **different**

Sounds like: this parrot

Picture: A pet shop owner explaining to a customer, "This parrot is different from this parrot."

Other forms: Disparity *(noun);* disparately *(adv)*

34

DISPERSE (dis-PERSE) *verb* — spread around; scatter

Sounds like: this purse

Picture: A woman taking lollipops from her purse and throwing them to eagerly awaiting children.

Other form: Dispersion *(noun)*   Note: Don't confuse with "disburse," which means "to pay out."

DISSENT (dis-SENT) *verb* — to disagree, especially with the majority, or with an authority

Sounds like: this scent

Picture: A crowd gathered in the capital of an unknown country. The king has just announced a "national scent" to go along with the national flag and national flower. The scent is lemon, and government workers have begun spraying the entire country with furniture polish. Many in the crowd disagree with the decision, holding up signs that say, "This scent is a lemon."

Other forms: Dissent, dissension *(nouns)*

DISSOLUTION (dis-so-LOOSH-un) *noun* — separation into parts; the process of dissolving

Sounds like: this solution

Picture: A chemist comes into the lab with a beaker of liquid. "This solution," she says, "must be separated into two parts." Then she pours half into one flask and half into another.

Other form: Dissolve *(verb)*

DISTENDED (dis-TEND-ed) *adj* — swollen; extended

Sounds like: this tendon (a tendon connects muscle to bone)

Picture: A man and woman are playing tennis. The match is several hours old when the man approaches the net with a very sad face and an elbow that's swollen to seven times its normal size. "I'm sorry, but I'll have to stop. It's this tendon. It swells up every time I play."

Other forms: Distend *(verb)*; distension or distention *(noun)*

DIVERGENCE (dye-VERR-jence) *noun* — the act of splitting off into different directions

Sounds like: diver gents

Picture: Two gentlemen diving from the same diving board, but in different directions. (Onlooker: "We're likely to get diverging accounts of this dive from the judges.")

Other forms: Diverge *(verb)*; divergent *(adj)*

DIVERSE (dye-VERSE) adj — different; various

Sounds like: dye furs

Picture: The father rabbit has dyed his seven children different colors. He explains to his wife: "I dyed their fur so they all look different. Now we can tell them apart."

Other form: Diversity (noun)

DOGMATIC (dawg-MAT-ik) adj — sticking to widely-accepted beliefs, even when faced with contrary evidence; closed-minded

Sounds like: dog medic

Picture: A medic (military doctor) arguing with a dog. The medic is insisting that there is no scientific proof that dogs can talk. The dog replies, "I think you're ignoring some important evidence."

Other forms: Dogma, dogmatism (nouns)

DOLEFUL (DOLE-full) adj — extremely sad

Sounds like: doll full

Think of: Doll full of tears. Picture a doll that cries and has a very sad expression.

Connect with: Dolorous, doldrums, and condolences

ECCENTRIC (ek-SEN-trik) adj — different from most, especially in personality or behavior

Sounds like: accent Rick

Picture: An old man named Rick who sits in a rocking chair on the sidewalk in front of his house and speaks in a different accent every five minutes. (The neighbors think he's a little weird.)

Other form: Eccentricity (noun)

ECLECTIC (ee-KLEK-tik) adj — choosing from many different sources; carefully selective

Looks like: electric

Picture: Two women talking in the kitchen. The visitor notices bills from six different electric companies for the same month. She asks about it. Her friend explains: "I like the electric heat I get from Eastwest Utilities, but I think the electricity from Superior Power is better for cooking. The lights are a little brighter since I started using Con Everyone Electric & Gas. And it just seems that the refrigerator keeps things colder with Central Illuminating. And then there's the hair dryer, and the VCR..."

Other forms: Eclectically (adv); eclecticism (noun)

EFFACE (ee-FACE) *verb* — erase

Sounds like: the face, and rhymes with erase

Picture: A penny that has been worn from use, so that Lincoln's face has been erased.

Note: Don't confuse with deface, which means to mar or disfigure.

EFFERVESCENCE (eff-er-VEH-sense) *noun* — **the quality of being bubbly or full of life**

Sounds like: ever pheasants

Picture: A large field surrounded by trees. The field is crowded with pheasants who are running around singing, dancing, and blowing enormous bubbles with those gigantic plastic rings and large pans of soap suds. Two beavers look on, one saying to the other, "Ah, pheasants, ever pheasants. So bubbly. So full of life... Well, let's get back to work."

Other forms: Effervescent *(adj);* effervescently *(adv)*

EFFICACY (EF-ih-kuh-see) *noun* — **the ability to produce desired results**

Sounds like: Effie can see

Picture: A little girl named Effie has been legally blind since birth. But today her eye doctor has presented her with a special pair of glasses, and when she puts them on she can see quite well. "I believe you'll be happy," says the doctor, "with the efficacy of these eyeglasses."

Other forms: Efficacious *(adj);* efficaciously *(adv)*

ELATED (ee-LAY-ted) *adj* — **extremely happy; overjoyed**

Sounds like: eel ate Ted

Picture: Mother eel to father eel: "Dear, I'm so happy! Baby eel ate Ted this morning! It's the first time he's eaten in weeks!" Father eel: "That's great, honey, but Ted was my brother. So now you're elated and I'm lugubrious." (Eels talk like that.)

Other form: Elation *(noun)*

ELOQUENCE (ELL-oh-kwence) *noun* — **powerfully effective speech**

Sounds like: elephants

Picture: The Republican National Convention. Thousands of Republicans have gathered in the convention hall to hear the guest speaker, an elephant (the party's mascot). Everyone in the hall has dressed up in elephant costumes. Elephant signs and posters are everywhere. "I'm all ears," says one member of the audience. "Many believe he's the best speaker in the country. And I'm told that once you hear one of his speeches, you never forget it."

Other forms: Eloquent *(adj);* eloquently *(adv)*

EMBELLISH (em-BEL-lish) *verb* — to make more beautiful; decorate; adorn

Sounds like: M bell fish

Picture: A young girl showing her mother how she's decorated the fish in their goldfish bowl. The fish have bells hanging from their bodies, and each of the bells has the letter 'M' on it. "Look, Mommy," says the girl, "M Bell Fish!" "Oh, they're beautiful," says the mother, "and if they ever jump out of the bowl, we'll be able to hear them flopping around on the floor! Let's go decorate the hamsters!"

Other form: Embellishment *(noun)*

EMULATE (EM-yoo-late) *verb* — imitate

Sounds like: Em, you're late

Picture: Emily is being scolded by her mother for getting home late: "Em, you're late." Standing right behind Emily is her younger brother, who says, "I'm late too, Mom, because I want to be just like Em."

Other form: Emulation *(noun)*

ENDEMIC (en-DEMM-ik) *adj* — native to a particular country or among a particular group

Sounds like: end emic

Think of: A country where everyone gets a strange illness called Emic Disease. Symptoms include swollen eyebrows, wrinkled kneecaps, and a kind of a sneeze-cough-hiccup that keeps sufferers (and their families) awake for weeks at a time. One day, the entire population gathers to protest the government's apathy about the disease. Ten thousand people with swollen eyebrows and wrinkled kneecaps fill the capital city and, between sneeze-cough-hiccups, they chant, "End Emic."

ENDORSE (enn-DORSE) *verb* — promote; recommend

Sounds like: end horse

Picture: A horse salesman saying to a customer, "I recommend the end horse."

Other form: Endorsement *(noun)*

ENERVATE (ENN-er-vate) *verb* — sap the strength; weaken

Sounds like: enter wait

Picture: A man attempting to get onto an elevator. The elevator operator tells him to enter, but every time he tries, the operator tells him to wait. After ten tries, the man is exhausted. "Enter, wait. Enter, wait." he says. "I'm drained. I think I'll take the stairs."

Other forms: Enervation *(noun);* enervative *(adj)*

ENHANCE (enn-HANTS) *verb* — **intensify; improve**

Sounds like: in hands

Picture: A man and woman have locked themselves out of their car. As the man encourages her, the woman manages to insert a wire hanger through the key chain inside the car and pull the keys out through the slightly open window. With the keys in her hands she says, "Well, this should enhance our chances of getting home."

Other form: Enhancement *(noun)*

ENIGMA (en-IGG-muh) *noun* — **mystery; puzzle**

Sounds like: an egg, Ma

Picture: A woman calling her mother from the maternity ward of a hospital, where she's just given birth to something unexpected: "This is hard to explain, but it's an egg, Ma." As she speaks, she glances over to the large egg in the crib next to her bed.

Other form: Enigmatic *(adj)*

ENMITY (ENN-mit-tee) *noun* — **mutual hatred**

Sounds like: enemy tee

Picture: Two people who completely hate each other are on the golf course together. They are about to tee off at the 'Enemy Tee,' where hostile players face each other with golf clubs and keep swinging until one of them has to be carried away. (Says one observer to another at the Enemy Tee, "This gives a whole new meaning to the term 'Grand Slam' event.")

Connect with: Amity *(noun)* — friendship. It's easy to tell these two words apart, because 'enmity' looks like 'enemy.'

EPHEMERAL (ee-FEM-er-al) *adj* — **temporary; short-lived**

Sounds like: F. M. mural

Picture: An artist, known by just his initials ("F.M."), who paints murals that fade away very soon after he completes them.

Other form: Ephemerally *(adv)*

ERADICATE (er-AD-ih-kate) *verb* — **remove completely and permanently; exterminate**

Sounds like: a rat, a crate

Picture: Your house is infested with rats and you would prefer that it weren't, so you call an exterminator. He comes over the next day with a bunch of crates. You watch with some curiosity as he spreads the crates all over the house. You look for traps, poison, spray guns, but you see none of that stuff. Just crates. So you ask him what's up. "The rats love these crates," he explains. "You put a crate out, a rat will go inside and close the lid. Nobody knows this, actually, I discovered it. But it's true. The thing is, each rat wants its own crate. If you have a rat, I bring in a crate. A rat, a crate. Fifty rats, fifty crates. I come back tomorrow and take them all away forever and you'll never even know they were here."

Other forms: Eradication *(noun)*; eradicable *(adj)*

ERRATIC (er-RAT-ik) *adj* — **unpredictable; differing from what is normal or expected**

Sounds like: ear attic

Picture: A house. The owner has installed giant ears on either side of the house, up near the attic. The neighbors across the street are looking at the ears and discussing the owner of the house. One neighbor: "He's always been kind of unpredictable, but this is strange, even for him."

Other form: Erratically *(adv)*

Note: Don't confuse with "erotic," which has to do with sex.

ERUDITION (err-yoo-DISH-un) *noun* — **the knowledge acquired through many years of study**

Sounds like: every edition

Picture: A student visiting his professor's office, where the walls are lined with many books. "Professor," asks the student, "have you read all these books?" The teacher responds: "Every edition."

Other forms: Erudite *(adj)*; eruditely *(adv)*

ESOTERIC (ess-oh-TERR-ik) *adj* — **known to, or understood by, a limited group of people**

Sounds like: it's so Derek

Picture: A group of men and boys attending a convention for people named Derek. Everyone at the Derek Convention is wearing a name tag that says, "Hello, My Name Is Derek," and they're all standing around talking about famous Dereks in history, telling Derek jokes, and thinking about the things that Dereks think about. An onlooker (named Jeffrey) says to a friend, "Don't ask me what they're talking about. I haven't understood one word they've said since I got here. It's all so, I don't know, it's so Derek."

Other form: Esoterica *(noun)*

ETHEREAL (ee-THEER-ee-ul) *adj* — heavenly; fine; delicately beautiful

Sounds like: eat cereal

Picture: A beautiful angel with platinum hair, delicately smooth skin, and a glowing face comes down from the sky to tell everyone how to achieve such a heavenly state: "Eat cereal."

Other forms: Etherealness *(noun);* ethereally *(adv)*

EULOGIZE (YOO-luh-jize) *verb* — to praise highly; to extol

Sounds like: your large eyes

Remember: In our culture, a eulogy is most often a speech given at a person's funeral. So picture the brother of the person who has died, speaking "to" his sister at her funeral (he's really speaking to the congregation, telling them about her). "You were the best sister anyone could hope for. You were sensitive, and understanding, and always willing to go out of your way to help someone in need. But what I'll always remember about you is your large eyes, filled with love and laughter."

Other forms: Eulogy *(noun);* eulogistic *(adj)*

Note: The prefix "eu-" almost always means "good." Look up eugenics, euphony, and euphoria in the dictionary, and see EUPHEMISM below.

EUPHEMISM (YOO-fuh-miz-um) *noun* — a word or phrase that's used to make an unpleasant idea sound better

Sounds like: you from prison

Picture: A woman asking a man, "You from prison?" The man, in a prison uniform, says he prefers "the big house."

Other forms: Euphemistic *(adj)*, euphemistically *(adv)*

EVASIVE (ee-VAY-siv) *adj* — tending to avoid giving direct answers

Looks like: Eva's hive

Picture: A bumble bee has flown his date, Eva, home. But she lives in a condominium of hives and doesn't want him to know which one is hers. "So," he says, "which hive do you live in, Eva?" "Oh, one of those over there," she answers evasively. "Well, anyway, I better get some rest. Give me a buzz some time."

Other forms: Evade *(verb);* evasiveness *(noun)*

The following words begin with "ex". "Ex" sounds like "eggs," so in order to remember many of these words, we will create characters, situations, and stories involving eggs.

EXACERBATE (ex-ASS-er-bate) *verb* — **to make a bad situation worse**

Sounds like: eggs as her bait

Picture: A woman is fishing from a rowboat, using hard-boiled eggs as bait. Nearby, in another rowboat, is her doctor. He's worried about her cholesterol level, which is already too high. "She's eating fish. And to make matters worse, she's using eggs as her bait. She's going to exacerbate the problem."

Other form: Exacerbation *(noun)*

EXALT (egg-ZAWLT) *verb* — **raise in rank; elevate; praise**

Sounds like: eggs salt

Picture: Hard-boiled eggs worshipping a salt shaker. As they glorify the salt, it is raised into the air, elevated by their praise.

Other forms: Exalted *(adj)*; exaltation *(noun)*

EXPUNGE (ex-PUNJ) *verb* — **erase**

Sounds like: x sponge

Picture: A sponge that erases everything it touches.

EXPURGATE (EX-per-gate) *verb* — **to remove offensive words, ideas, or symbols; censor**

Sounds like: eggs pure gate

Picture: Someone has painted obscene graffiti on a gate. The eggs who live next-door are horrified, and immediately repaint the gate to return it to its pure condition.

Other forms: Expurgation *(noun)*; expurgatory *(adj)*

EXTEMPORANEOUS (ex-tem-por-AY-nee-us) *adj* — **done without planning; improvised**

Sounds like: eggs temp or rains

Picture: You're watching the six o'clock news, waiting for the weather report (you're planning a family back-to-nature camping trip tomorrow and you want to know if you'll need to bring an umbrella for the VCR). But the regular weatherperson is sick and her substitute is this egg who doesn't have a script or any idea what he wants to say. It sounds like this: "If we look at the map, we see a lot of big letters and numbers. Let's see, what do you suppose this "82" means? It could be the temp. Or, the chance of rain, or the amount of rain we might get tonight. Hey, let's all just wait and see what happens. No point in standing here trying to guess what the weather will do, right? Now back to you, Katie and Bob..."

Other form: Extemporaneously *(adv)*

EXTOL (ex-TOLE) *verb* — **praise**

Sounds like: eggs toll

Picture: A giant egg working as a toll collector. The driver must praise the egg before he's permitted to pass through the gate.

Other form: Extolment *(noun)*

EXTRANEOUS (ex-TRAY-nee-us) *adj* — **unnecessary; irrelevant**

Sounds like: extra trains

Picture: A small town with a small population and a small train station. Each morning exactly two people wait on the platform. At 8:05, the train pulls into the station, the two passengers board, and the train leaves the empty platform behind. At 8:09 another train arrives, but there's nobody there. At 8:14 another train arrives. At 8:20, still another train pulls into the empty station. This continues all day long, eight trains every hour for the only two people in the whole town who commute to work.

Other forms: Extraneously *(adv)*; extraneousness *(noun)*

EXTRICATE (EX-trik-ate) *verb* — **to free from a trap or difficult situation; to disentangle**

Sounds like: eggs truck Kate

Picture: Kate works on a chicken farm. One day, Kate is loading eggs onto the back of a truck when the driver is attacked by a crazed chicken. Startled, the driver puts the truck into gear and takes off, bouncing at high speed down the dirt road into town. Meanwhile, Kate has fallen headfirst into the back of the truck and has been knocked unconscious, buried beneath boxes of eggs, which have toppled onto her. Arriving at his destination, the driver runs to the back of the eggs truck, discovers Kate, and frees her from her trap. (Kate is angry. To find out what she and the driver say to each other, see PALTRY.)

Other forms: Extrication *(noun)*; extricable *(adj)*

EXUBERANT (ex-ZOO-burr-ent) *adj* — **uncontrollably joyous**

Sounds like: ex-zoo bear aunt

Picture: A grizzly bear who had left the zoo returns to visit his aunt. When they see each other, they are both very happy, hugging and dancing and singing for many hours.

Other forms: Exuberance *(noun)*; exuberantly *(adv)*

FALLACIOUS (fuh-LAY-shuss) *adj* — **false; misleading**

Sounds like: full ashes

Picture: Father and son on the lawn in front of the son's house. Dad says, "Be sure to always clean the ashes out of the fireplace." He is unaware that the ashes have filled the fireplace and the entire chimney and are spilling out onto the roof. "Don't worry, Dad," says the young man. "I clean it out every day."

Other forms: Fallacy *(noun);* fallaciously *(adv)*

FASTIDIOUS (fass-TID-ee-uss) *adj* — **difficult to please**

Sounds like: fast hideous

Picture: A decorator showing her client many kinds of wallpaper. Every time she holds up a sample, the client says, "Hideous!" The faster she shows the samples, the faster the client says, "Hideous!"

Other forms: Fastidiousness *(noun);* fastidiously *(adv)*

FERVOR (FER-ver) *noun* — **strong passion**

Sounds like: fever, or forever

Picture: A young man telling his girlfriend how much he loves her. He speaks with an intensity of passion that seems to have no limits. "Ophelia, my love for you is like a hurricane at sea, wild, uncontrollable! I'm drowning in it! It's swallowing me up, tearing me to pieces, dashing me against the rocks. I am shredded by passion! I am consumed by fever! A fever that will last forever!" (The young woman is shocked. Finally she says, "My goodness, Rudy, it sounds like you should be going out with a nurse.")

Other forms: Fervidness *(noun);* fervidly *(adv)*

FICKLE (FIK-uhl) *adj* — **lacking loyalty; unpredictably changeable; erratic**

Rhymes with: pickle and nickel

Picture: A little girl and her teacher. The teacher is holding up a picture of a pickle and a picture of a nickel and has asked the girl which she likes better. The girl says she likes pickles better. Then she says she likes nickels better. She continues to alternate, changing her mind every few seconds.

Other form: Fickleness *(noun)*

FLACCID (FLASS-id) *adj* — **lacking firmness; soft; limp**

Sounds like: flat Sid

Picture: A jellyfish named Sid. Like all jellyfish, Sid has no bones in his body, so he is unable to maintain any shape. When he's dropped onto a table, he becomes completely flat.

Other forms: Flaccidly *(adv);* flaccidity *(noun)*

44

FLAGRANT (FLAY-grent) *adj* — **openly and obviously evil; glaring; conspicuous**

Looks like: flag rent

Picture: A man and woman parading on the sidewalk in front of their apartment building. Each carries a flag that says, "We have no complaints about this building or our apartment, but we aren't going to pay our rent and we don't care who knows it."

Other forms: Flagrantly *(adv)*; flagrancy *(noun)*

FLEDGLING (FLEJ-ling) *noun* — **beginner**

Sounds like: fresh wings

Picture: A newly-hatched bird trying to fly with fresh (new) wings. The bird can't fly because he's a beginner.

FLIPPANCY (FLIP-an-see) *noun* — **treating a serious situation with arrogant humor or disrespect**

Sounds like: flip and see

Picture: A man sits in the electric chair. Just minutes earlier, a storm knocked out power and now one of the guards asks if the electricity is back on. The prisoner smiles casually and gestures to the large switch on the wall next to the chair: "Just flip and see."

Other forms: Flippant *(adj)*; flippantly *(adv)*

FOMENT (foe-MENT) *verb* — **to stir into action; rouse; incite**

Sounds like: foam mint

Picture: A man who has covered his face with foam mint (a mint-scented shave cream). He runs through the streets, trying to stir the other men to follow his lead and finally shave off their beards. "It's time to unite," he yells, "and remove the whiskers that keep us from seeing who we really are!"

Other form: Fomentation *(noun)*

Note: Don't confuse with: "ferment," which is a chemical process.

FORESIGHT (FOR-site) *noun* — **the ability to see ahead, anticipate, or predict**

Sounds like: four sight

Picture: A woman who wakes up every morning at four o'clock and has a vision in which she can "see" the events of the coming day. As she explains it, "I can yell at my kids for things they haven't even thought about doing yet!"

Other forms: Foresighted *(adj)*; foresee *(verb)*

FRUGAL (FROO-gull) *adj* — **careful with money; thrifty**

Sounds like: few gulls

Picture: The man who wasted his inheritance on gulls (see PRODIGAL) has a brother. This brother received the same inheritance, but when he met the seagull salesman, he only bought a few gulls.

Other forms: Frugality *(noun);* frugally *(adv)*

FULMINATE (FULL-min-ate) *verb* — **to explode, either with sound or anger**

Sounds like: full men ate

Picture: Three large men at a picnic. They ate and ate until they were full, then the full men ate some more, until they literally exploded. After witnessing this, the men's wives blew up in anger.

Other form: Fulmination *(noun)*

I DON'T CARE WHO PUTS THEIR HAND OUT... WE'RE NOT FORKING OVER ONE MORE DIME!

COAT CHECK

FURTIVE (FER-tiv) *adj* — **sneaky; secretive**

Sounds like: fur tip

Picture: Husband and wife are about to leave a fancy restaurant. They have just picked up her fur from the coat check room and he's complaining about the prices of the meals, the fact that they have to pay for parking, the cost of the babysitter, etc. Meanwhile, his wife is sneaking back to the coat check girl to slip her a dollar.

Other forms: Furtiveness *(noun);* furtively *(adv)*

FUTILE (FYOO-til) *adj* — **hopelessly ineffective; useless; in vain**

Sounds like: few tile

Picture: Two men on a roof. They're professional roofers, which is why they're up there and which means they're supposed to know how to estimate how many tiles they'll need to do a certain roof. But they underestimated and now they're trying to figure out how to stretch the few tiles they have left to cover about forty square feet of roof area. "It's hopeless," says one. "Too few tiles."

Other forms: Futility *(noun);* futilely *(adv)*

NFRTHRMPF MSDSMNR THMPF

GARBLED (GAR-bulled) *adj* — **changed so much that the original meaning has been distorted; scrambled**

Sounds like: gargled

Picture: A man talking and gargling at the same time. His friend is trying hard to understand the message, but it's too distorted to comprehend.

Other form: Garble *(verb)*

GARISH (GAIR-ish) *adj* — **flashy; gaudy**

Looks like: car fish

Picture: A fish swimming in the ocean. This fish has fins like a '58 Chevy, with flashy chrome trim and pinstriping; its scales are two-tone metallic. When it moves past other fish, it turns on a set of blinking lights that act as turn signals, and sounds a horn that plays the theme from "Flipper."

Other forms: Garishly *(adv)*; garishness *(noun)*

GARNER (GARR-ner) *verb* — **collect; gather; accumulate; earn**

Sounds like: gardener

Picture: A gardener showing the many ribbons she has collected for her prize-winning flowers.

Other form: Garner *(noun)*

GARRULOUS (GAIR-uh-luss) *adj* — **very talkative; loquacious**

Sounds like: Gary Loose

Think of: A talkative man named Gary Loose Lips. Gary's lips are so loose, he can't stop talking for a second. Gary is wearing a pair of low gray shoes, which are also talking (see LOQUACIOUS).

Other form: Garrulity *(noun)*

GENIAL (JEE-nee-ul) *adj* — **friendly; gracious; kind**

Sounds like: Genie Al

Picture: A Genie named Al has just come out of his bottle. He is extremely friendly and accommodating, wanting very much to please everyone around him.

Other form: Geniality *(noun)*

GERMANE (jer-MAYNE) *adj* — **relevant; fitting**

Looks like: Germany

Picture: A courtroom scene. The lawyer asks the witness on the stand, "What's the capital of Germany?" The judge interrupts: "Counselor, I don't see how that question is relevant to this case."

GIRTH (GERTH) *noun* — **the measured distance around an object (its circumference)**

Rhymes with: birth

Picture: A pregnant woman, very wide around the middle.   47

GLUTTON (GLUT-tin) *noun* — **a person who consumes huge quantities of food or drink; someone with great endurance**

Looks like: a combination of "glue" and "button"

Picture: A big casserole of glue and buttons. Someone seated at the dinner table is devouring an enormous amount of this stuff, for some reason.

Other forms: Gluttony *(noun);* gluttonous *(adj)*

GRAVITY (GRAH-vih-tee) *noun* — **seriousness**

Sounds exactly like: gravity, the word referring to the force that holds us to the Earth.

Picture: An astronaut has landed on some distant planet with very powerful gravity. The force is so strong that the astronaut has been flattened by it (a serious situation).

Other forms: Grave *(adj);* gravely *(adv)*

GREGARIOUS (greh-GAIR-ee-uss) *adj* — **sociable; extroverted; enjoying companionship**

Sounds like: Greg, Gary, and us

Picture: A man and woman are getting ready to leave for vacation. As the husband carries his suitcase down the stairs, he sees that two friends are seated in his living room. His wife explains that she's inviting everyone they know to go on vacation with them. "Well, so far it's Greg, Gary, and us," she says. "But I'm still waiting to hear from Audrey, Fred, and Nora Jean. And Fred's going to call his brother, and Audrey's asking everyone in her building..."

Other forms: Gregariously *(adv);* gregariousness *(noun)*

GULLIBLE (GULL-ih-bull) *adj* — **easily deceived**

Sounds like: gully bull

Picture: A bull has fallen into a gully, obviously tricked by the other bulls, who are laughing.

Other form: Gullibility *(noun)*

HACKNEYED (HAK-need) *adj* — **unoriginal; trite**

Sounds like: hat kneed

Picture: Two women with fancy hats on their knees commenting on a third woman with baseball caps on her knees.

HAMPER (HAM-purr) *verb* — **interfere with movement or progress**

Sounds like: hamper (as in clothes hamper)

Picture: A gigantic clothes hamper parked in the middle of a highway, causing traffic to back up for miles.

HAPHAZARD (hap-HAZ-erd) *adj* — **without plan or direction**

Sounds like: hop Hazel (also notice the word "hazard")

Picture: Hazel plans to hop across the state of North Dakota. As she gets ready to go, a reporter asks what her plan is, how many maps she has, and how she intends to deal with the hazards out there. Hazel: "Plans? Maps? Who needs them? I'm just going. If I get lost, I'll go a different way. And if I run into any hazards, I'll hop around them. Well, here I go. See you when I get somewhere."

Other forms: Haphazardly *(adv);* haphazardness *(noun)*

HARANGUE (her-RANG) *noun* — **a long, lecturing speech**

Sounds like: her gang

Picture: A meeting of a women's gang. The leader is delivering an endless lecture about the importance of wearing helmets on the road. (One member interrupts: "But we're driving stationwagons.")

Other form: Harangue *(verb)*

HARBOR (HAR-ber) *verb*— **to provide shelter or refuge; hide**

Sounds exactly like: harbor (the body of water)

Picture: While fishermen prowl around on the ocean, an organization called "The Undersea Railroad," run by large turtles and seals, helps get fish into the harbor, where they can hide until it's safe.

Other form: Harborer, harborage *(nouns)*

HARDY (HARD-ee) *adj*— **bold; brave; capable of withstanding harsh conditions**

Looks like: hard Y

Picture: The letters of the alphabet are in a log cabin, holding a contest to see who can stand out in the cold for the longest time. Now 25 of them have come in to sit near the fire. Several letters are looking out the window at the Y, standing in the snow. It's below zero and windy, but Y doesn't move. "He is one hard letter," says R. "Hey, U, why don't you go out there and tell him to come in?" "Not me," answers U. "We vowels are too soft for this kind of weather."

Other forms: Hardiness *(noun);* hardily *(adv)*

Don't confuse with "hearty," which means "enthusiastic."

HEDGE (HEJ) *verb* — to avoid giving a definite or clear answer, thereby escaping responsibility or blame

Sounds exactly like: hedge

Picture: A wealthy woman is questioning her gardener about the horribly trimmed hedge in front of her mansion. The gardener, not wishing to be castigated, avoids the question with vague answers: "The hedge? I don't recall who trimmed it this week. I mean, yes, I am the only gardener, but maybe one of the neighborhood kids sneaked into the toolshed and used the clippers. I'm not saying that's what happened, but then again, who can know for sure...?"

Note: "Hedge" means to beat around the bush!

HEED (HEED) *verb* — notice; pay attention to

Sounds exactly like: he'd

Picture: A boy is about to leave for college. His mother is trying to hide her sadness with an endless string of warnings (addressed to her husband): "He'd better drive carefully. And he'd better call the minute he gets there. And he'd better be listening to me. And he'd better brush his teeth after dinner. And he'd better go to bed early tonight. That's all I'm going to say, but he'd better pay attention. And he'd better study every day. Is he listening to me?"

Other form: Heed *(noun)* — as in, "to take heed."

HEINOUS (HAY-niss) *adj* — shockingly evil

Sounds like: hang us

Picture: Three men standing on the steps of the gallows, three nooses dangling from the cross-bar. One of the men says to the sheriff, "Our crimes were heinous. All you can do is hang us."

HERESY (HEHR-eh-see) *noun* — an opinion expressed in defiance of generally accepted ideas

Sounds like: her a C

Picture: A college philosophy class. Two students are discussing the grade a third student received on a paper: "He gave her a C just because she titled her paper, 'Socrates Was An Idiot.'"

Other forms: Heretic *(noun);* heretical *(adj);* heretically *(adv)*

HIATUS (high-ATE-us) *noun* — gap; interruption; a break in the continuity of a process; a pause

Sounds like: Hi, Atus

Picture: A group of bricklayers building a wall. As the foreman, a man named Atus, inspects the five-foot-high wall, he comes to a gap — a place where the wall is only a foot high, as if the bricklayer assigned to that portion had stopped working several hours ago. Just then he hears someone yell out, "Hi, Atus!" and turns around to find the missing bricklayer lying down on a lounge chair. The brick layer explains, "I needed a little break."

50

HIERARCHY (HY-er-ar-kee) *noun* — a group of people in authority, ranked in order of power; a sequential listing

Sounds like: hire Archie

Picture: The executive board meeting of a large corporation. The chairman is standing at a flip-chart showing the company's chain of command, beginning with him at the top. Each of the boxes below the chairman on the chart has the name of a vice president or assistant vice president, except one box, which is blank. The chairman is saying, "I want you to hire Archie for this position. I think he'd fit very well into the hierarchy of the company."

Other form: Hierarchical *(adj)*

HOMAGE (OMM-ij) *noun* — respect paid to someone or something; tribute; honor

Looks like: home age

Picture: A very, very, very old house. The house has been restored to its original appearance and is beautifully decorated. From miles around, real estate agents, historians, and tourists come to visit the old house and show their respect. "I don't even know the home's age," says one visitor, "but I feel I should pay homage to it."

HOMOGENEOUS (ho-mo-JEEN-ee-us) *adj* — the same throughout; consistent; uniform

Sounds like: home of genius

Picture: A genius is being studied by a team of scientists. They're trying to determine if anything about her home life has contributed to her amazing mental abilities. When they arrive they find that the home of this genius is remarkably consistent: all of the rooms are exactly the same size, the walls are all the same color, and every piece of furniture is the same height and style. In addition, the light bulbs are all 75 watts, the air is always maintained at 70 degrees, and every book in the house contains exactly 384 pages. "Hmmm," says one of the scientists, "maybe the home of a genius needs to be homogeneous."

Other forms: Homogeneousness *(noun);* homogeneously *(adv)*

HYPERBOLE (hi-PURR-boe-lee) *noun* — extreme exaggeration

Looks like: Hyper Bowl

Think of: Two things: the use of the word, "hype," meaning to heavily promote something, thus exaggerating its attraction, and football's Super Bowl, which is usually hyped beyond belief. Now combine these two ideas and imagine a "Hyper Bowl," a game that requires the two teams to out-exaggerate each other. The players are lined up, face-to-face. Someone from one side says, "You don't have a chance against us. We won our last game by forty-seven touchdowns." Someone from the other team responds, "By the time we're finished, they'll have to pick you guys out of the grass with tweezers."

Other form: Hyperbolic *(adj)*

YOU KNOW I ALWAYS HAVE YOUR BEST INTERESTS IN MIND.

HYPOCRITE (HIP-oh-crit) *noun* — **an insincere person; one who pretends to have feelings he doesn't really possess**

Sounds like: hippo crit

Picture: A hippopotamus smiling at his friend, even as he steals his wallet.

Other form: Hypocritical *(adj)*

IDOLATRY (eye-DOLL-uh-tree) *noun* — **the worship of objects or people as gods**

Sounds like: a doll, a tree

Picture: People had been coming from all over town, and now they're arriving from other states, to see the man who worships the doll in the tree. He has placed one of his daughter's dolls high up in a maple tree on his front lawn, and every morning at 7 a.m. he kneels on the damp grass and bows before the doll, praying and asking for forgiveness.

Other forms: Idolater *(noun)*; idolize *(verb)*; idolatrous *(adj)*

IMBUE (im-BYOO) *verb* — **to fill, as with a strong dye or a strong feeling**

Looks like: I'm blue

Picture: A worker at the dye factory has fallen into the blue vat. When he pulls himself out, his clothes and skin are completely imbued with the dye. "How do you feel?" his co-workers ask. He responds simply, "I'm blue."

IMMINENT (IMM-uh-nint) *adj* — **about to take place; happening soon**

Sounds like: in a minute

Picture: A farmer and his son discussing the tornado that's supposed to be on its way. The father, listening to the radio: "They say the tornado is imminent. When do you think it will get here?" The son, looking out the window, sees the dark funnel on the horizon. "In a minute," he says.

Other forms: Imminently *(adv)*; imminence *(noun)*

IMMUTABLE (im-MYOO-tah-bull) *adj* — **unable to change**

Looks like: a mute table

Picture: Two chairs have been trying, without success, to strike up a conversation with a table. As the table sits silently (mutely), one chair says to the other, "It's no use. Tables just don't talk. They never have and I guess they never will."

Other forms: Immutability *(noun)*; immutably *(adv)*

IMPAIR (im-PARE) *verb* — **weaken in strength or value**

Looks like: I'm pair

Picture: An exhausted pear seated at his desk, holding the telephone receiver upside-down and talking into it.

Other forms: Impairment *(noun)*; impaired *(adj)*

IMPASSE (IM-pass) *noun* — **a situation from which you cannot escape; stalemate**

Sounds like: him pass

Picture: Two cars face each other, front-bumper-to-front-bumper, on a narrow road. There isn't enough room for them to go around each other, and neither driver is willing to back up, so they sit. An observer on the side of the road watches the conflict, listening to each driver yell, "I refuse to let him pass!"

Don't confuse with: Impassive (see below)

IMPASSIVE (im-PASS-iv) *adj* — **without feeling; expressionless**

Looks like: Impasse (refer to the situation described under IMPASSE, above)

Picture: The person watching the impasse between the two drivers is looking on impassively. He is totally unconcerned with how the conflict will be resolved and, as the drivers grow angrier and angrier, he remains calm and expressionless (impassive).

Other forms: Impassively *(adv)*; impassivity *(noun)*

IMPEDE (im-PEED) *verb* — **get in the way; hinder**

Looks like: I'm Pete

Picture: Pete walks out onto the track while a women's relay race is going on. Just as two racers are about to exchange the baton, he walks between them and says to one, "I'm Pete."

Other forms: Impedance, impediment *(noun)*

IMPETUOUS (im-PETCH-oo-us) *adj* — **making quick decisions and taking sudden action; hasty; impulsive**

Sounds like: in pet shoes

Picture: Wife comes home with the family sheepdog. Husband is watching TV and looks over to see that the dog is wearing very stylish shoes on all four paws. "I just bought them without thinking," wife explains. "They were there in the window, we were walking by, we both liked them, so I bought them. I know it was impetuous, but hey, he does have that kennel dance next Friday."

Other forms: Impetuosity *(nouns)*; impetuously *(adv)*

53

IMPOSTOR (im-POSS-ter) *noun* — **pretender**

Looks like: I'm Postor

Picture: A man named Mr. Postor is about to receive a special award that includes a $25,000 prize, many gifts, and the praise and respect of thousands of people. Suddenly, another man bursts into the room yelling, "Wait! I'm Postor! He's a fake!"

IMPUDENCE (IMP-yoo-dense) *noun* — **rudeness; insolence**

Sounds like: in pew dance (a pew is a seat or bench in a church)

Picture: It's Sunday morning and the church is filled. The minister is about to begin her sermon when suddenly a man jumps up in his pew and performs a wild dance. The churchgoers are shocked, to say the least, at his rudeness and lack of consideration for others.

Other forms: Impudent *(adj)*; impudently *(adv)*

Note: Don't confuse with "imprudence," which means "a lack of wisdom" (see PRUDENT).

INADVERTENT (in-ad-VER-tent) *adj* — **unintentional**

Sounds like: in at her tent

Picture: An army troop camping out during an overnight hike. One of the men accidentally walks into the tent of a female officer. Furious, she throws him out. (One observer: "So he made a mistake. What's the big deal?" Second observer: "It's the seventh time today he's made that mistake.")

Other forms: Inadvertently *(adv)*; inadvertence *(noun)*

INANE (in-NANE) *adj* — **silly; insignificant**

Looks like: insane (without the "S")

Picture: A man reads a letter from his psychiatrist, then cries to his wife: "He says I'm insane!" When he becomes hysterically upset, she takes the letter and reads it. "No, it says 'inane,'" she tells him. "It's nothing to worry about. You're just being silly."

Other forms: Inanity *(noun)*; inanely *(adv)*

INAUGURATE (in-AWG-yer-ate) *verb* — **begin; induct into**

Sounds like: in Aug. you're eight

Picture: The Mid-Childhood Club, made up of children between the ages of eight and thirteen. The president is speaking to a new group of kids, all of whom will be celebrating their 8th birthday on August 1st. The date is July 31: "In Aug. you're eight, and each of you will be welcomed into the Mid-Childhood Club as official members."

Other forms: Inauguration *(noun)*; inaugural *(adj)*

INCESSANT (in-SESS-ent) *adj* — **continuous; endless**

Sounds like: in says ant

Picture: An ant hill just before a storm. One ant stands at the door and says, "In! In! In!" over and over and over as an endless stream of ants pours into the shelter.

Other forms: Incessantly *(adv)*; incessancy *(noun)*

INCHOATE (ink-OH-ett) *adj* — **not yet fully developed**

Sounds like: ink oh-eight

Picture: A tank, such as one you would see at a winery. But this is an inkery, where ink is made and stored. The ink in one particular tank has not aged enough, so is not yet ready for use. The tank is labeled, "Ink 0-8."

INCITE (in-SITE) *verb* — **arouse to action; stir up; foment**

Sounds like: ignite

Picture: A small country that has been controlled by a foreign nation for many years. One day, on the tenth anniversary of the country's takeover, a woman runs through the streets of the capital. She calls for action, urging the citizens to fight for their freedom. Like a spark falling into dry grass, she ignites a fire of anger among the people, and it quickly grows into a blazing revolution.

Other forms: Incitement, incitation *(nouns)*   Note: Don't confuse with "insight," the ability to perceive.

INCOMPATIBLE (in-kum-PAT-a-bull) *adj* — **incapable of existing together in peace**

Sounds like: in combat with Bill

Picture: A woman has left her husband and gone to stay with a friend. "It's no use," she says. "Every day I find myself in combat with Bill. We just cannot get along."

Other forms: Incompatibility *(noun)*; incompatibly *(adv)*

INCONGRUOUS (in-KON-groo-uss) *adj* — **out of place**

Sounds like: in Congress

Picture: The U.S. Capitol (Congress) with something unexpected in the middle of the picture.

Other forms: Incongruity *(noun)*; incongruously *(adv)*

INCORRIGIBLE (in-KORR-ij-uh-bull) *adj* — **impossible to correct, control, or discipline**

Sounds like: in car itch a bull

Picture: A bull family out for a drive in their Ford Taurus. One of the children in the back seat has put fleas and ticks under his father's seat. The father, trying to drive, is squirming from the itch. Mother Bull scolds her son: "You are absolutely incorrigible!"

Other forms: Incorrigibility *(noun);* incorrigibly *(adv)*

INCREDULOUS (in-CREJ-oo-luss) *adj* — **unwilling or unable to believe**

Sounds like: ink red, you lose!

Picture: A man is playing roulette at a casino. He's been at it a while, winning, losing, winning, losing. Now he's put all of his money, including his car keys and the deed to his house, on "25 Black." The attendant spins the wheel and talks as the wheel slows down: "looking for black ink, looking for black ink, looking for black... and ink's red, you lose!" The man stares at the wheel for a long time. "I can't believe it," he says. "I just can't believe it!"

Other forms: Incredulity *(noun);* incredulously *(adv)*

Note: An object or event is <u>incredible</u>; the person observing it is <u>incredulous</u>. Also, connect with all words containing the root "cred," such as credence, credulous, credibility, credentials, and credit; all have to do with "belief."

INDICT (in-DITE) *verb* — **charge with a crime; accuse**

Sounds like: in tight

Picture: A man has his right arm stuck in the cash slot of an automated teller machine at the bank. An alarm has sounded and the police are about to come in. "I'm really in tight here," he thinks. "I'm sure they're going to charge me with attempted robbery."

Other form: Indictment *(noun)*

INDIGENT (INN-deh-jint) *adj* — **very poor**

Sounds like: Indy Gent

Picture: A very poor man named Indy Gent. His clothes are tattered and dirty and he has few or no possessions. It may be that he's so poor because he's also indolent. (See INDOLENT.)

Other forms: Indigence, indigent *(nouns)*

Note: Don't confuse this word with "indigenous," which means "native or inborn." Or "indignant," which means "angry."

INDOLENT (INN-doe-lent) *adj* — **lazy**

Connect with: Indigent. Picture Indy Gent, who is very poor. Now think of why he's so poor. Maybe he's extremely lazy and doesn't want to work. So he's indigent because he's indolent. To distinguish between the two similar sounding words, remember that indolent has an "L" in it, for lazy.

Other forms: Indolence *(noun)*; indolently *(adv)*

INDUCE (in-DOOSE) *verb* — **cause to happen; bring about**

Sounds like: in deuce

Picture: Two well-known tennis players are engaged in a long and difficult match. One player falls behind in the final game, then suddenly manages to lure his opponent into a series of mistakes (he's caused the mistakes to happen). Now they're in deuce.

Other forms: Inducement *(noun)*; inducible *(adj)*

INERT (ih-NERT) *adj* — **lacking movement; inactive; sluggish**

Sounds like: in dirt

Picture: Fossils of animals found deep in the dirt. They have remained motionless and unchanged for thousands of years. They are inert.

Other forms: Inertness, inertia *(nouns)*; inertly *(adv)*

INFALLIBLE (in-FAHL-ih-bull) *adj* — **incapable of making a mistake**

Looks like: in fall a bell

Picture: A tall tower in the middle of town. In the tower there is a bell that rings just once a year, at the moment summer ends and fall begins. Whether the season starts on September 20, 21, or 22, the bell always rings exactly on schedule, to the second. It never makes a mistake.

Other forms: Infallibility *(noun)*; infallibly *(adv)*

Alternate approach: Just think of "in<u>fail</u>able."

INFAMY (INN-fuh-mee) *noun* — **a bad reputation; notoriety**

Sounds like: in for me

Picture: A lifelong criminal is complaining about the news media. "They've got it in for me," he says. "And why? What have I done? Some bank robberies, two or three dozen murders, a kidnapping here and there. So where did I get this terrible reputation?"

Other forms: Infamous *(adj)*; infamously *(adv)*

INFER (in-FER) *verb* — to figure out, based on given information; conclude; deduce

Sounds like: in fur

Picture: A scientist finds a baby seal on the shore. When he picks up the animal, he notices that the seal's fur is coated with oil. From this information (the oil in the fur), the scientist concludes that there has been an oil spill somewhere in the area.

Other forms: Inference *(noun);* inferential *(adj)*

Note: Infer doesn't mean "to imply" or "to suggest." When you infer something, you <u>take in</u> information.

INFILTRATE (IN-fil-trayt) *verb* — penetrate by passing through gaps; enter secretly and become established, such as a spy might do in an enemy organization

Sounds like: infield rate

Picture: The owner of a major league baseball team is upset. Someone has leaked to the press very secret information about what she's paying the infielders on the team (infield rate). "There's a spy among us," she tells her board of directors. "Someone has infiltrated this organization and is telling our financial business to the newspapers. Now all the outfielders will want raises."

Other forms: Infiltration *(noun);* infiltrative *(adj)*

INGENUOUS (in-JEN-yoo-us) *adj* — naive; unsophisticated; inexperienced

Looks like: ingenious

Remember: "Ingenuous" and "ingenious" look almost exactly alike, so it's easy to confuse them. Take a good long look at both words. Learn to distinguish between them. (In a sense, they're opposites.)

Now, imagine a brilliant person, such as Thomas Edison, who has come up with an *ingenious* invention, such as the light bulb. Now also imagine that Mr. Edison is pretty unsophisticated, or *ingenuous*, when it comes to business. He might say something like, "Okay, so it lights up. Big deal. Who's going to buy it? Everyone has candles. Maybe I'll just give it to my cousin Phil, and if he wants to market it, let him make a few bucks." Mrs. Edison replies, "Tom, you're so ingenious, but you're also ingenuous."

Other forms: ingenuousness *(noun);* ingenuously *(adv)* Connect with: Disingenuous ("shrewd")

INNATE (in-NATE) *adj* — having a quality that arises from within, rather than learned or acquired from the outside; native; inborn

Sounds like: Inn Eight

Picture: A woman and man are looking through a guidebook in search of a country inn for their vacation. "I like inn number eight," says the woman, pointing at a number on a map in the book. "It doesn't have a swimming pool, or a fancy menu, or a golf course nearby. But there seems to be something about this place. It has an innate quality, a charm the others are missing."

Other forms: Innateness *(noun);* innately *(adv)*

Note: Be careful not to confuse "innate" with "inane." But <u>do</u> connect it with "inherent."

INNOCUOUS (in-NOK-yoo-uss) *adj* — **harmless; inoffensive**

Sounds like: inn octopus

Picture: A couple arriving for a weekend stay at a country inn. The innkeeper points out the dining room, the fireplace in the library, and the live octopus in the parlor. "Oh, don't worry about him," the host says to the startled guests. "He's harmless."

Other forms: Innocuously *(adv);* innocuousness *(noun)*

INNOVATION (in-no-VAY-shun) *noun* — **A new idea or product; a new way of doing something that is so much better, it causes others to copy it**

Sounds like: an ovation

Picture: An inventor talking to the producer of a TV show. He has invented a device that simulates the sound of a crowd giving an ovation. The producer considers it a wonderful innovation, because it eliminates the need for live people, who could be unpredictable in their responses to the show.

Other forms: Innovative *(adj);* innovate *(verb)*

INSCRUTABLE (in-SKROO-tuh-bull) *adj* — **mysterious**

Sounds like: on scooter bull

Picture: Archeologists have discovered drawings on the walls of a cave. The drawings are thousands of years old and clearly show a bull riding a scooter. "We shall call these drawings, "On Scooter Bull," says a scientist. "But we may never know what they mean."

Other forms: Inscrutability *(noun);* inscrutably *(adv)*

INSIPID (in-SIP-id) *adj* — **dull; flat; without sparkle or flavor**

Sounds like: in! sip it!

Picture: A young child, sick with the flu. Her mother is trying to get her to drink some flat ginger ale to calm the child's upset stomach. "In! she says. "In! Sip it! I know it has no flavor. Just sip it."

Other form: Insipidly *(adv)*

INSOLENT (IN-so-lent) *adj* — **rude; haughty**

Sounds like: insulin (a hormone produced by the pancreas)

Picture: A meeting of the body's internal organs. Each speaks in turn. Suddenly the pancreas starts yelling about how important he is, and how the body wouldn't be able to absorb carbohydrates without his insulin, and how he should be thanked for the work he does. ("There he goes again," says the liver. "Spouting insulin and insolence. I hope he doesn't get the stomach upset.")

Other forms: Insolence *(noun);* insolently *(adv)*

INSOLVENT (in-SOL-vent) *adj* — **unable to pay bills; bankrupt**

Sounds like: in Sol's vent

Picture: The owner of a small business walks to the bank to deposit his money. Right in front of Sol's Ripoff Emporium he trips, dropping the bag of money down a vent in the sidewalk. When he looks down the vent, he sees the money, but it's now in Sol's basement. Sol is a crook and will never give it back. "All my money's in Sol's vent!" he cries. "Now I won't be able to pay my bills!"

Other form: Insolvency *(noun)*

INTERMITTENT (in-ter-MIT-tint) *adj* — **occurring at intervals; periodic; not constant or continual**

Sounds like: in her mitten

Picture: A little girl stands outside in the falling snow. Every once in a while, a snowflake lands in her mitten. She never knows when it will happen, but she knows it will happen again soon.

Other forms: Intermittently *(adv);* intermission *(noun)*

INTRACTABLE (in-TRACK-tah-bull) *adj* — **stubborn; immovable**

Looks like: in-track table

Picture: A table wedged between railroad tracks. Two people are trying to move it. "It's no use," says one. "It refuses to budge."

Other forms: Intractability *(noun)*; intractably *(adv)*

INTRINSIC (in-TRIN-zik) *adj* — **located within the very nature of an object or person; inherent**

Sounds like: in train sick

Picture: A man and woman on a train. The man looks as if he's about to either throw up or pass out. Meanwhile, his wife explains to the conductor, "No, it isn't the motion or the speed or the noise, because he doesn't get sick on cars or airplanes or roller coasters. There's some quality intrinsic to trains that makes him feel sick."

Other form: Intrinsically *(adv)*

INVERT (in-VERT) *verb* — **turn upside down or inside out; reverse position**

Looks like: invent

Picture: A scientist named Dr. Bert Invert. Dr. Invert has invented a device that turns objects upside down, regardless of their size or weight. When you enter Dr. Invert's lab, you notice that tables, chairs, desks, and lamps are all upside down. "I was going to invert the entire building," he says, "but the plumber advised against it."

60   Other forms: Inversion *(noun);* inverted and invertible *(adj)*

IRASCIBLE (ihr-RASS-ih-bull) *adj* — **easily angered**

Sounds like: erase a bull

Picture: A very tempermental artist has been trying to draw a bull for several days, but every version looks worse than the one before. As he gets angrier and angrier, he screams at himself, "Draw a bull, erase a bull. Draw a bull, erase a bull!"

Other forms: Irascibleness *(noun);* irascibly *(adv)*

IRONY (EYE-rah-nee) or (EYE-er-nee) *noun*
— **an unexpected outcome, or the use of a word that is the opposite of its literal meaning.**

Sounds like: iron knee

Picture: Basketball player who wished for knees like iron. Instead, he got irons on his knees.

Other forms: Ironic *(adj);* ironically *(adv)*

MAYBE IT'LL HELP HIM WITH THE FULL COURT PRESS

IRRESOLUTE (eer-REZ-uh-loot) *adj* — **indecisive; unsure**

Sounds like: ear razor loot

Picture: A man, dressed as a giant ear, in the audience of "Let's Make A Deal." He has to decide whether to keep the electric razor he's won or go for the loot behind door number 3. "I'll keep the razor. No, wait, I'll take the loot. I don't know, the razor or the loot? How much time do I have? Can I call you in the morning?"

Other forms: Irresoluteness *(noun) ;* irresolutely *(adv)*

IRREVERENT (eer-REV-rent) *adj* — **disrespectful**

Sounds like: ear Reverend

Picture: In the lobby of the church hangs a photograph of the Reverend. One of the members of the congregation, obviously lacking in respect for this particular member of the clergy, has painted enormous ears on the Reverend's picture.

Other forms: Irreverence *(noun);* irreverently *(adv)*

Connect with: Revere (opposite)

JARGON (JARR-gun) *noun* — **specialized language used by a particular group**

Sounds like: jar gone

Picture: Policeman questioning the burglary victim: "So you're saying that the alleged perpetrator unlawfully removed from your domicile one wide-mouthed vessel made principally of earthenware?" Victim pointing to empty shelf: "No, what I'm saying is that my jar is gone."

JAUNDICE (JAWN-diss) *noun* — **yellow color; or, envy or resentment**

Sounds like: enjoying this

Picture: The little third-grade girl couldn't wait for her mother to come to Parents' Night at her school so she could show off her artwork. Everyone in the class had to draw and then paint something yellow. The girl drew pencils and bananas and daffodils, painted them all yellow, wrote "Yellow Stuff" at the top, and taped it to her classroom wall. But when her mother came into the room, she stopped at another girl's work (called "Color My World Yellow") and admired it so much she couldn't tear herself away to look at her daughter's painting. "I'm sorry, dear," the mother said, "but I'm enjoying this. I'll see yours later." The little girl could only look on in envy.

Other form: Jaundiced *(adj)*

JAUNTY (JAWN-tee) *adj* — **lively; perky; sprightly**

Sounds like: jointy

Picture: A wooden puppet dancing around, each of his <u>joints</u> swinging freely and rhythmically.

Other forms: Jauntiness *(noun);* jauntily *(adv)*
Note: Don't confuse with "jaunt" (a short trip).

JEOPARDY (JEP-er-dee) *noun* — **the threat or possibility of danger**

Sounds exactly like: Jeopardy! (the TV show)

Picture: The set of the Jeopardy! show. The three contestants are standing behind their podiums. Suddenly, the player in the lead finds himself in possible danger because of the resentment of one of his fellow contestants.

Other form: Jeopardize *(verb)*

JETTISON (JET-ih-sun) *verb* — **to throw overboard; to discard**

Sounds like: jet a son

Picture: A jet plane ten thousand feet up and running out of fuel. The captain tells the flight attendants to open one of the emergency doors and get rid of all unnecessary cargo in order to make the plane lighter. One of the passengers offers to throw his teenage son out if it would help.

JOCULAR (JOCK-yoo-ler) *adj* — **joking; playful; jesting; witty**

Sounds like: Dracula

Picture: Count Dracula is working as a stand-up comedian, using the name Count Jocular: ("...So he says to me, 'I can't take blood from a stone.' I say, I know, I've been trying for years!")

Other forms: Jocularity *(noun);* jocularly *(adv)*

Connect with: "Jocose" and "jocund," which have similar meanings to "jocular." Just about any unfamiliar word you come across that begins with "joc" will have something to do with "joke."

JUBILANT (JOO-bill-ent) *adj* — **filled with joy**

Sounds like: gerbil ant

Picture: A gerbil (like a hamster) and an ant are very happy to see each other after a long time. They hug and dance and smile and kiss each other. ("I'm sorry I haven't called," says the gerbil, "but I do about twelve miles a day on that wheel and it really wears me out." "I know what you mean," replies the ant, "I've been working with a bunch of carpenter friends on a wood-frame house a few blocks from here, and that's been keeping me busy for months. But I'm so happy to see you!")

Other forms: Jubilation *(noun);* jubilantly *(adv)*

JUDICIOUS (joo-DISH-uss) *adj* — **wise; making good decisions**

Sounds like: Jew dishes

Picture: Passover is an important holiday for Jewish people. For those who celebrate it in the most traditional way, special dishes are used for the food — dishes that are used only for Passover. Imagine a family that's about to begin the Passover ceremony. The man says to his wife, "I think you made a wise decision by taking out your grandmother's old dishes this year. They make the table look beautiful!"

Other forms: Judiciousness *(noun);* judiciously *(adv)*

JUNCTURE (JUNK-sher) *noun* — **point in time, especially a crucial one; joint or connection**

Sounds like: junk chair

Picture: You are one of seven people playing musical chairs. Everyone is circling the six chairs and the music has just stopped. You look at the two chairs you have stopped between; one looks okay but the other seems to be falling apart. It is time to make a crucial decision: do you take a chance with the junk chair, which is closer, or do you lunge for the sturdier-looking chair?

JUXTAPOSE (juk-stah-POZE) *verb* — to place side-by-side

Sounds like: just suppose

Picture: A woman in her living room, listening to the interior decorator, who is holding a painting of a shark and a photograph of the woman's three small children. "Just suppose we do this," he says. (He wants to place the pictures side-by-side, but when he does so, it looks as though the shark is about to swallow the children.)

Other form: Juxtaposition *(noun)*

KINDLE (KIN-dil) *verb* — to start a fire; ignite; arouse

Sounds like: candle

Picture: A young man is serving dinner to his date, who is seated opposite him at an elegant table. He lights one of the candles, hoping the romantic atmosphere will kindle feelings of love in the woman. Instead, he accidentally knocks the candle over onto the tablecloth, kindling a small but disruptive fire.

Other form: Kindling *(noun)* — thin twigs and sticks used to start a fire in a fireplace.

KINETIC (kin-ETT-ik) *adj* — in motion; active

Sounds like: Connecticut

Picture: You're on the space shuttle orbiting the Earth. As you pass over the northeastern United States, you notice the entire region is absolutely still, except in Connecticut, where everything is in motion. Trees are hopping, buildings are sliding from block to block, and mountains are spinning like inverted tops.

LACONIC (luh-KONN-ik) *adj* — quiet; of few words; terse

Sounds like: Lake Onnic

Picture: A small lake hidden in the woods in upstate Maine, where even the birds sing only one note at a time. A man rows a boat across the lake; a woman rows her boat from the opposite side of the lake. When they pass, he says, "Morning." She replies, "Bye." And so it is on Lake Onnic, where the people tend to keep things inside and have very little to say to each other.

LAMENT (luh-MENT) *verb* — express sorrow; complain

Sounds like: lamb mint

Picture: A flock of sheep has wandered into town, looking for one of their lost members. As they pass a restaurant, they notice "Lamb with Mint Jelly" on the menu. Immediately, their imaginations run wild and they convince themselves that the lamb on the menu is the lamb they've been looking for. Overcome with grief and sorrow, they all sit on the sidewalk in front of the restaurant, moaning and wailing.

Other forms: Lament, lamentation *(nouns)*; lamentable *(adj)*; lamentably *(adv)*

LANGUISH (LANG-gwish) *verb* — lose energy or motivation; become weak or depressed

Sounds like: Lang wish

Picture: A young man named Lang. He graduated from college eight months ago and has been lying around ever since. Every day he says to his dog, lying on the floor next to him, "I wish I could find the energy to go get a job, but I'm just too tired today."

Connect with: Languor *(noun)*; languorous *(adj)*

LATENT (LAY-tint) *adj* — existing but inactive, such as a certain quality; dormant or still; invisible

Looks like: Latin

Picture: A woman who learned Latin when she was very young, then ignored it for the next seventy years. Throughout her adult life, Latin words and phrases would occasionally race through her mind and roll around in her mouth, but she would never express them. Her fluency in the language still resided within her, but she stifled it, so that her Latin remained dormant — a latent ability.

Other form: Latency *(noun)*

LAUD (LAWD) *verb* — praise; worship; extol

Sounds like: lord

Picture: A minister preaching in a church in Alabama. "Laud," he says in his Alabama accent, "you are truly great! Laud, we worship and extol you. Laud, we offer you our praise!"

Other forms: Laudatory, laudable *(adj)*; laudably *(adv)*

LEGACY (LEGG-uh-see) *noun* — something inherited, either from an ancestor or from the past itself

Sounds like: leg I see

Picture: The nephew is waiting patiently as his uncle's will is being read. Finally it is announced that he has inherited a single leg of an antique chair. "A leg, I see," he says.

Note: A legacy could be a physical gift, such as money, or something abstract, such as knowledge.

LETHARGIC (leh-THAR-jik) *adj* — tired; sluggish; drowsy

Sounds like: leather chick

Picture: A young chicken is trying to run around the barn, but she's too tired. The problem is that when she hatched she was covered with leather instead of feathers, and the combination of heat and the weight of the leather has drained her of all her energy.

Other forms: Lethargy *(noun)*; lethargically *(adv)*

LEVITY (LEV-ih-tee) *noun* — **lightness; playfulness; jocularity**

Sounds like: levitate

Picture: A magician is levitating his assistant; that is, he is causing her to float in mid-air without ropes or wires. Normally, magicians are very serious about this part of their act, asking the audience to keep silent, dimming the lights, and behaving as if the assistants were in some sort of danger. However, this particular magician is quite the opposite. As he levitates the young woman, he dances around, smiles, and tells jokes. "Excuse my levity, folks, but I'm just trying to get a <u>rise</u> out of her!"

LIONIZE (LIE-uh-nize) *verb* — **to put someone onto a pedestal; to treat with great respect**

Sounds like: lion eyes

Picture: In the jungle, a group of lions has decided to honor a leopard for his courage, strength, and skill. He has what they call "lion eyes," and has therefore been chosen to be an honorary lion, making him a great celebrity in the jungle.

LISTLESS (LIST-less) *adj* — **tired; sluggish; lacking drive**

Sounds exactly like: list less

Picture: Doctor speaking to a tired-looking patient: "When did you start feeling this way?" Patient: "I found this list in a magazine, 'Ten Ways to Stay Energetic.' But I lost the list last week, and I've been exhausted ever since."

Other forms: Listlessness *(noun);* listlessly *(adv)*

LOATH (LOATH) *adj* — **reluctant; unwilling**

Sounds like: load

Picture: You've just finished watering and combing your prize-winning lawn. A dump truck filled with rocks and boulders pulls up in front of your house. The driver gets out and tells you that he's supposed to dump the load onto your lawn. You, of course, are loath to let him do so.

LOATHE (LOATH) *verb* — **to hate**

Sounds exactly like: loath

So how do you tell "loath" and "loathe" apart? It's easy: just look at the end of the word "loathe," which means "to hate." Loathe has the letters H-A-T-E in it (they're jumbled a bit, but they're there). So if you can spell hate, that's what it means.

Other forms: Loathsomeness, loathing *(nouns);* loathsome *(adj);* loathsomely *(adv)*

LOFTY (LAWF-tee) *adj* — **at a great height; elevated; noble**

Sounds like: loft tea

Picture: A 50-story building. At the very top is a loft, which is being used by a group of philosophers for a daily tea party and conversation. On the street, a man is sweeping the sidewalk and talking to a passerby, who is looking up toward the loft. "They're up there drinking fancy tea," says the man, "and discussing their lofty ideas."

Other form: Loftiness *(noun)*

LOQUACIOUS (low-QUAY-shuss) *adj* — **talkative**

Sounds like: low gray shoes

Picture: A pair of low gray shoes. Both shoes are talking.

Other forms: Loquaciousness *(noun)*; loquaciously *(adv)*

LUCID (LOO-sid) *adj* — **easy to understand; transparent; clear-thinking**

Sounds like: Lou said

Picture: A lecture, featuring a speaker named Lou, has just ended. As members of the audience leave the auditorium, one of them can be heard to say, "I understood everything Lou said. It was all so clear."

Other forms: Lucidity *(noun)*; lucidly *(adv)*

LUDICROUS (LOO-dih-kruss) *adj* — **absurd; ridiculous**

Sounds like: Lou to cross

Picture: A 24-lane super highway. Cars are racing by at 80 mph in every lane. Lou stands at the edge of the highway, waiting for a break in the traffic so he can cross the road. "Lou," yells a friend from a passing car, "it's ludicrous to think you can ever get across. There hasn't been a break in this traffic since 1986!" ("Well, isn't that ludicrous?" Lou says to himself. "Does that guy really think I can hear him with all these cars going by?")

Other forms: Ludicrousness *(noun)*; ludicrously *(adv)*

LUGUBRIOUS (loo-GOOB-ree-uss) *adj* — **mournful**

Sounds like: Lou Goober's

Picture: Lou Goober's Funeral Home. Lou, standing out front, is a sad-looking guy.

Other forms: Lugubriousness *(noun)*; lugubriously *(adv)*

67

MAGNANIMOUS (mag-NAN-ih-muss) *adj* — **big-hearted; generous; forgiving; noble**

Sounds like: my Nanny Moose

Picture: Young moose telling her classmates about her grandma, Nanny Moose, "the most generous, wonderful, kind-hearted moose in the whole world."

Other forms: Magnanimously *(adv);* magnanimity *(noun)* Note that the root "magn" means great or large, while "anim" pertains to the mind, soul, or spirit. Thus, big-hearted.

MAGNATE (MAG-net) *noun* — **a person of great power**

Sounds like: magnet

Picture: A country populated by paper clips and other small, metal objects. The country's ruler is a large, powerful magnet. The magnet has total influence and control over the citizens.

The root "mal" means "bad." For the next four words, we will examine the words and actions of a most unpleasant person. His name is Mal.

MALEDICTION (mal-uh-DIK-shun) *noun* — **evil speech; curse**

Sounds like: Mal eviction

Picture: Mal hasn't paid his rent in five months and has just received an eviction notice. The letter explains that he must either pay all back rent within 30 days or be kicked out of his apartment. Furious, he calls his landlady on the phone and screams and curses at her, calling her the most horrible names he can think of.

Other form: Maledictory *(adj)*

MALEFACTOR (mal-uh-FAK-ter) *noun* — **person who tries to hurt others; criminal**

Sounds like: Mal he faxed her

Picture: Mal is still upset about the eviction notice (see MALEDICTION) and plans to send his landlady a letter bomb. But instead of mailing the letter bomb, he decides to fax it to her. Of course, she receives a harmless letter, the fax machine blows up in Mal's face, and he grows even angrier (see MALICE).

Other form: Malefaction *(noun)*

MALICE (MAL-iss) *noun* — **a desire to cause harm or suffering**

Looks like: Mal ice

Picture: Mal is on the roof of his building with a gigantic block of ice, which he's about to drop onto his landlady's head.

Other forms: Malicious (adj); maliciously *(adv)*

MALIGN (muh-LINE) *verb* — to say evil or harmful things about someone; defame; vilify

Sounds like: Mal lying

Picture: Mal's landlady has taken him to court for non-payment of rent. On the witness stand, Mal pretends to be an innocent victim. Instead of fighting, he decides to malign his landlady by lying about her. He says that she called him up and said horrible things to him on the phone, faxed him a letter bomb, and even tried to drop a block of ice on his head.

Other form: Malignant *(adj)*

MALLEABLE (MAL-ee-uh-bull) *adj* — able to be reshaped by force; pliable; impressionable

Sounds like: mallet-able

Picture: A woman who collects sculpture, but whose taste in art changes every day. After purchasing dozens of sculptures, only to quickly grow tired of them, she decides to buy one made of raw clay. She also goes to the hardware store and gets herself a mallet (little hammer). Now, when she gets bored with the sculpture's shape, she beats it with the hammer until it looks like something else. "It may not be marketable as art," she says, "but it sure is malleable."

Other form: Malleability *(noun)*

MARRED (MARD) *adj* — spoiled, scratched, blemished

Sounds like: Mars

Picture: The surface of Mars, which is pitted with craters.

Other form: Mar *(verb)*

MEAGER (MEE-ger) *adj* — small in size or amount; thin; weak

Sounds like: me grrr

Picture: A small, frail puppy has just been given his bowl, which contains a tiny amount of food. As gigantic human feet walk by, the puppy expresses his anger over the meager dinner: "Me grrrr!"

Other forms: Meagerness *(noun);* meagerly *(adv)*

MEANDER (me-ANN-der) *verb* — **wander in a carefree manner; follow a winding course; ramble**

Sounds like: me and her

Picture: A young man, newly in love, walks down a path along a winding river, his arm around his girlfriend. They walk slowly, mindlessly, he singing a song he makes up as they go along:
"Me and her,
My girl Wanda,
We love to wander,
Me and her..."

Other forms: Meandering *(adj);* meander *(noun)*

MELLIFLUOUS (mel-IF-loo-uss) *adj* — **smooth; sweetly flowing**

Sounds like: Mel leaf loose

Picture: Mel is an opera singer. His voice is so smooth, so sweet, that it makes the trees shiver and lose their leaves. (A man raking the leaves might say: "I never did like opera!")

Other forms: Mellifluously *(adv);* mellifluent *(adj)*

MENDACITY (men-DAH-sih-tee) *noun* — **a lie; a false statement**

Sounds like: mend a city

Picture: Grandpa and Grandson sitting on the porch. Grandpa is telling one of his famous stories: "It was 1929, I guess. I was living in California, a place called Menda City. Well, one morning an earthquake hit, and I'm talking about a real whopper. Every building was down. People had no place to live, they were living in the streets, businesses had to close. And here I was, the only person in town who knew how to build anything. So I started teaching some of the others and we got to fixing things up. I directed the whole project, which was called 'Operation Mend A City.' Get it? Mend A City. Menda City. See how that worked? Anyway, soon we had all brand new buildings and life got back to normal, and the people were so grateful, they made me mayor and wouldn't let me leave office for the next twenty years..." (Grandson thinking to himself, "I get sent to my room for telling stories like this.")

Other forms: Mendacious *(adj);* mendaciously *(adv)*

METICULOUS (meh-TIK-yoo-luss) *adj* — **extremely careful about details**

Sounds like: me ticklish

Picture: Man who works in a pillow factory. His job is to stuff the feathers into the pillows. He has to be careful because he's very ticklish and if he doesn't do his job exactly right, he ends up on the floor, laughing. ("But if I do a good job," he says, "I get to take a nap on my coffee break.")

Other form: Meticulously *(adv)*

MINUTE (my-NOOT) *adj* — **very small in size**

Sounds like: my newt

Think of: A newt, which is a small salamander. A young boy is holding out his hand and saying to his older sister, "This is my newt." The sister, looking at the tiny spot on his hand, thinks he said "This is minute."

Other form: Minuteness *(noun)*

Connect with: Minutiae, which means minor details.

MISCONSTRUE (miss-kun-STROO) *verb* — **misunderstand; interpret incorrectly**

Sounds like: Miss Kahn's Two

Picture: Woman on the telephone at a restaurant called Miss Kahn's Two. She's speaking to a friend who thought they were supposed to meet at Miss Kahn's on the other side of town. Here's how they each misconstrued what the other was saying:

Woman 1: "I'm going out for dinner tonight."
Woman 2: "So am I. Where are you going?"
Woman 1: "I'm going to Miss Kahn's."
Woman 2: "Really? I'm going to Miss Kahn's, too!"
Woman 1: "Oh, okay. I'll see you there!"

MITIGATE (MITT-uh-gate) *verb* — **make less severe; mollify**

Sounds like: middle gate

Picture: Return to the scene of the man cursing the gate (see CASTIGATE), but now the middle gate has calmed and soothed the angry man, to the relief of the first gate.

MOLLIFY (MOLL-ih-fie) *verb* — **lessen anger; soothe; placate**

Sounds like: Molly Fly

Picture: Molly Fly follows the Village Fly around; she soothes the feelings of the people he has upset (see VILIFY).

MONOLOGUE (MONN-oh-log) *noun* — **a long, uninterrupted speech by one person**

Sounds like: man on a log

Picture: A man standing on a log in the woods. His audience is a group of rabbits, foxes, mice, deer, raccoons, and birds, and they all look very tired from listening to his endless monologue: "...And so, dear friends, let me remind you once again that we must be careful not to miss the forest for the trees..."

MOROSE (mawr-OSE) *adj* — depressed

Sounds like: more oats

Picture: Depressed horse at a bar. The bartender asks, "More oats, pal?"

Other forms: Moroseness *(noun)*; morosely *(adv)*

MUNDANE (mun-DAYNE) *adj* — ordinary; earthly (not spiritual); practical; temporary

Sounds like: Monday

Picture: A weekly meeting of ghosts, gathering to discuss important matters of eternal and supernatural significance. However, one of the ghosts is only concerned about what day of the week it is. "Monday. Monday? Is today Monday? Our meetings are supposed to be held on Mondays. Shouldn't we check the calendar?" Another responds, "Clarence, we don't need to worry about such mundane matters."

Other form: Mundanely *(adv)*

MYRIAD (MEER-ee-id) *adj* — large number; many

Sounds like: Mary had

Think of: The song, "Mary Had A Little Lamb." Now imagine that this lamb grew up and had little lambs of her own. And then <u>they</u> all had little lambs, and so on, so that in a few years, Mary had thousands of little lambs. (They all still followed her to school. Luckily, she went to a large university.)

Other form: Myriad *(noun)*

NEFARIOUS (neh-FAIR-ee-uss) *adj* — extremely evil

Sounds like: no ferry is

Picture: A crazed, wicked modern-day pirate who attacks and plunders ferry boats filled with rush-hour commuters.

"No ferry is safe from me," he proclaims. Other form: Nefariously *(adv)*

NEGLIGENT (NEG-lih-jint) *adj* — careless in a situation that could result in harm; neglectful

Sounds like: negligee

Picture: Husband is upset. Wife came downstairs in the middle of the Christmas party in her negligee.
    He: "How could you be so careless?"
    She: "It was a simple mistake. What harm was done?"
    He: "What harm? Do you know how embarrassed I was? Do you know that my boss saw you wearing that negligee? Do you know that because of your neglect, I could lose my job?"
    She: "Do you know that your boss asked me if we'd invite him to our New Year's Eve party?"

72   Other form: Negligence *(noun)*

NEOPHYTE (NEE-oh-fite) *noun* — **beginner**

Sounds like: neo-fighter

Picture: A nervous young boxer who is about to get into the ring for the first time.

Connect with: Any words that begin with "neo." They always refer to something that is new.

NOCTURNAL (nok-TERN-il) *adj* — **active at night**

Sounds like: knock, turn, Al

Picture: The local chapter of the "Midnight Club," a group of people who only go out late at night. Al is a new member and doesn't know how to get into the club's secret building. A whispering voice from the intercom system tries to help him: "Give the official Midnight Club knock on the door, then turn the knob. Got it? Knock, turn, Al!"

Other form: Nocturnally *(adv)*

NOSTALGIC (nuh-STAL-jik) *adj* — **wishing for a return to the way things used to be; longing for the past; homesick**

Sounds like: nose tell cheek

Picture: A face with stylish eyeglasses perched on the nose. The nose looks over to one cheek and says, "I miss the <u>old</u> glasses."

Other form: Nostalgia *(noun)*

NOVELTY (NAH-vul-tee) *noun* — **something new or unusual**

Sounds like: novel tea

Picture: A teacup with a novel as a teabag. Or, novels pouring out of a teapot's spout.

Other form: novel *(adj)*

NUANCE (NOO-onts) *noun* — **slight degree; shade of difference**

Sounds like: new ants

Picture: A "new & used ant" lot. The "vehicles" are ants, the salesman and customer are anteaters. Salesman explains the subtle ways in which this year's model differs from last year's.

NULLIFY (NUL-ih-fy) *verb* — **remove or cancel all value or force; negate**

Looks like: null if Y ("null" means "having no value")

Picture: Nellie has the airplane ticket in her hand as she speaks to an airline representative. He tells her that the ticket is null and void if the letter Y appears at the top. She looks, and sure enough, there's a Y. The ticket's value has been nullified.

Other forms: Nullification *(noun);* null *(adj)*

NURTURE (NER-cher) *verb* — **provide care and support; nourish; train or educate**

Sounds like: nurse chair

Picture: The maternity ward of a hospital. In one corner of the nursery is the Nurse Chair. In this large rocker, the nurse sits to feed and talk to the infants, giving them love and nourishment. Here is also where the new mothers come to learn from this experienced nurturer about caring for their babies.

Other forms: Nurturer, nurturance *(nouns)*

The following nine words begin with the letters "ob". Because "ob" sounds like "Hobb," the pictures for all of the words will involve Mr. Hobb.

OBDURATE (OB-der-it) *adj* — **stubborn; unyielding**

Sounds like: Hobb door 8

Picture: Hobb and his wife are looking for a friend's apartment. When Hobb knocks on door #8 a strange man answers. "I'm sorry," says Hobb's wife. "We must have the wrong apartment." But when the man closes the door, Hobb knocks on it again, insisting that it's where his friend lives. No matter how many times his wife and the man at the door assure him that it's the wrong apartment, Hobb refuses to listen and keeps going back to it.

Other forms: Obdurateness *(noun);* obdurately *(adv)*

OBJURGATE (OBB-jur-gate) *verb* — **scold; castigate; denounce**

Looks like: Hobb jury gate

Picture: Hobb is on jury duty. He has just entered the enclosed area of the courtroom where the jury sits, but he's forgotten to close the gate. The judge scolds him: "Mr. Hobb, will you please close the jury gate! This is the third time I've had to remind you! How are you going to remember the details of this trial if you can't remember a simple thing like closing the gate?"

Other form: Objurgation *(noun)*

OBLITERATE (uh-BLIT-er-ate) *verb* — **remove or destroy completely; erase**

Looks like: Hobb litter ate

Picture: Hobb has just dropped some gum wrappers on the ground. When he rounds the corner he sees a police officer walking toward him. Hobb is afraid he'll get a ticket for littering, so he runs back around the corner and eats the wrappers! By the time the police officer arrives, the litter has been obliterated.

Other form: Obliteration *(noun)*

OBSCURE (obb-SKYOOR) *adj* — **hazy; unfamiliar; difficult to understand**

Sounds like: Hobb's cure

Picture: Patient coming out of Dr. Hobb's office. The patient's wife questions him about the visit:

> Wife: What did Dr. Hobb say?
> Patient: I'm not sure.
> Wife: Well, did he say it was curable?
> Patient: I think so, but maybe not. He was pretty vague.
> Wife: What's that prescription for?
> Patient: I have no idea. He told me, but I didn't understand.
> Wife: Is this Hobb's Cure? Send your patient home in a fog?
> Patient: It might be. How would I tell?

Other forms: Obscurely *(adv)*; obscurity *(noun)*

OBSEQUIOUS (ob-SEEK-wee-us) *adj* — **behaving like a meek, spineless servant; subservient; sycophantic**

Sounds like: Hobb's sequins

Picture: Hobb's brother and his wife are visiting for a few days. One night, Hobb walks into the living room and finds his brother, in his wife's sequin dress, standing on a chair. Seeing the surprised expression on Hobb's face, the brother explains: "She told me to put it on so she can see how it looks from a distance. I'd do anything for my wife, and this is such a little favor. Tomorrow afternoon I'm going to wear it to our favorite restaurant so she can see how it looks in the light there. She wants me to."

Other forms: Obsequiousness *(noun)*; obsequiously *(adv)*

OBSOLETE (obb-so-LEET) *adj* — **no longer usable; outdated**

Sounds like: Hobb so late

Picture: Hobb riding in a horse & buggy, arriving for an important meeting. His co-workers are annoyed at his lateness, and wonder why he's driving such an obsolete vehicle.

Other form: Obsolescence *(noun)*

75

OBSTINATE (OBB-stin-ett) *adj* — **stubborn; refusing to be persuaded**

Sounds like: Hobbs ten-eight

Picture: Hobb playing basketball with some of his friends. Hobb insists the score is ten-eight, even when assured by his opponents and his own teammates that the score is twelve-six. "Look," says Hobb, "I don't care that you all think it's twelve-six, or that we have spectators who agree with you, or that we have the game on videotape and that it shows the score to be twelve-six. I still say the score is ten-eight. Why should I change my mind?"

Other forms: Obstinacy *(noun);* obstinately *(adv)*

OBTUSE (obb-TOOSE) *adj* — **dull; blunt; unintelligent; lacking sharpness**

Sounds like: Hobb two's

Picture: Hobb as a young boy standing at the blackboard, where he has written "2 + 2 = 97." Not exactly a genius, poor young Hobb just doesn't see where he's gone wrong.

Other forms: Obtuseness *(noun);* obtusely *(adv)*

OBVIATE (OBB-vee-ate) *verb* — **eliminate the need for something; make unnecessary**

Sounds like: Hobb V-8

Picture: Hobb driving a very large, brand new car (with a V-8 engine) past his old horse & buggy (see OBSOLETE). Hobb tells the horse that he doesn't need him anymore.   Other form: Obviation *(noun)*

OMINOUS (OMM-in-uss) *adj* — **a sign of something unpleasant that's about to happen; inauspicious**

Sounds like: "Oh, my noose!"

Picture: A condemned man looking at the noose that will soon be placed around his neck. Growing extremely nervous, he says, "Oh, my noose!"

Other form: Omen *(noun);* ominously *(adv)*

ONEROUS (OWN-er-uss) *adj* — **burdensome; oppressive**

Sounds like: owner Russ

Picture: A man named Russ is scolding a teenager he's hired to wash and wax his expensive car: "Come on!" he yells. "Put some effort into it. Make that radio antenna shine!" ("Wow," thinks the exhausted young man. "This owner, Russ, is really creating a burden for me.")

Other forms: Onerousness *(noun)*; onerously *(adv)*

OPAQUE (oh-PAKE) *adj* — **too dark or thick for light to pass through**

Sounds like: oh cake

Picture: Right after the wedding reception, the newlyweds run to their car to leave for their honeymoon. They're surprised to find no "Just Married" sign on the back or bells hanging from the mirrors. But when they get into the car they notice the entire windshield has been covered by a thick, white substance, which they obviously can't see through. When they look more closely they say, "Oh, cake!"

Other forms: Opaqueness, opacity *(nouns)*; opaquely *(adv)*

OPPORTUNIST (opper-TOON-ist) *noun* — **someone who takes advantage of the situation**

Sounds like: opera tunist (the man who tunes the instruments at the opera)

Picture: The lead singer faints and the opera tunist runs in to help: "I can sing! I'll take his place!"

Other form: Opportunistic *(adj)*

OPTIMIST (OPP-tih-mist) *noun* — **someone who always believes things will turn out okay**

Looks like: a combination of "optometrist" and "mist"

Picture: An optometrist (eye specialist) leading his family on a hike up the side of a mountain. The mist is heavy and they can't see anything, but he insists they'll make it: "I've developed these special glasses that help you see through mist. If we all put them on, I know we'll get to the top in a few minutes. And you know what else? I think there'll be a picnic lunch waiting for us up there. And soft chairs to sit on..."

Other forms: Optimistic *(adj)*; optimistically *(adv)*

OPULENCE (OPP-yoo-lence) *noun* — **luxury; wealth; riches**

Looks like: opal fence (opal is a precious gem)

Picture: We were visiting cousins in a wealthy part of the state. My brother and I wandered off and walked toward the lake, where we came upon a magnificent house in the woods. We saw six Rolls Royces parked in the long, circular driveway. The shrubs were sculpted to look like dollar signs. But the most amazing sight of all was the fence. It ran around the entire property and was made completely of opal. It glistened and shone in the afternoon sun, the brightest, most luxurious thing we had ever seen.

Other forms: Opulent *(adj)*; opulently *(adv)*

PACIFIST (PASS-uh-fist) *noun* — **person who refuses to fight**

Sounds like: pass a fist

Picture: Bully standing with his fist raised, threatening a smaller man. But the smaller guy refuses to fight and walks past the fist.

Other form: Pacify *(verb)*

Connect with: Pacific, pacifier, peaceful

PALTRY (PAWL-tree) *adj* — **worthless; insignificant, petty**

Sounds like: poultry

Remember Kate and the eggs truck? (See EXTRICATE.) Okay, so the driver goes to the back of the truck and rescues Kate. But she's very angry, and when he tries to explain that the crazed chicken made him drive off so wildly, Kate says, "Well, that's a poultry excuse!" (She means 'paltry,' or worthless, but the driver is too scared to correct her.)

Other form: Paltriness *(noun)*

THE WORLD'S MOST EXCELLENT GUNS

PARAGON (PAHR-a-gon) *noun* — **model of excellence; the best**

Sounds like: pair of guns

Picture: The world's most perfect guns.

PARITY (PAHR-ih-tee) *noun* — **equality or equivalence; balance among a group of rivals**

Looks like: party

Picture: A boy is having a birthday party at his house. On the same day, the girl next door is having her birthday party. Holding a pair of binoculars, the boy watches everything that happens at the other party, then runs to his mother and demands equality. "Her cake is chocolate with pink frosting. That's what I want. And a clown just showed up. Where's my clown? She has bigger balloons..."

Note: Don't confuse this word with "parody," which refers to an imitation that is meant to poke fun at the subject.

PARSIMONY (par-SIMM-uh-nee) *noun* — **stinginess; excessive frugality**

Looks like: parsley money

Picture: A woman at a fruit and vegetable stand, haggling with the owner about the price of parsley: "Look, I budget forty-nine cents a month for parsley, and that's all I'm going to pay for it."

Other form: Parsimonious *(adv)*

PARTISAN (PAR-tih-zin) *adj* — **blindly devoted to a cause or organization**

Sounds like: party sun

Picture: A member of an unknown country's military. He's been assigned to a secret mission by the ruling <u>party</u>: they want to put him in a rocket ship and send him to the <u>sun</u>. As any member of his party would be, he is honored. "Of course I will do it," he says. "It is a privilege. It is what every faithful party member waits for all his life. This will be my moment in the sun."

Other forms: Partisan, partisanship *(nouns)*

PAUCITY (PAW-sih-tee) *noun* — **too few; scarcity**

Sounds like: poor city

Picture: A poor city consisting entirely of slums. There is a scarcity of everything in this city: the citizens lack the things they need.

PECUNIARY (peh-KYOON-ee-er-ee) *adj* — **having to do with money; financial**

Sounds like: petuniary, or petunias

Picture: Petunias with dollar bills for flowers.

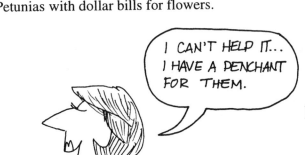

I CAN'T HELP IT...
I HAVE A PENCHANT
FOR THEM.

PENCHANT (PENCH-ent) *noun* — **a strong liking; attraction**

Sounds like: pendant

Picture: A woman with many pendants around her neck. She obviously has a strong liking for pendants.

PENURY (PEN-yer-ee) *noun* — **extreme poverty; destitution**

Sounds like: pen Yuri

Picture: The same guy named Yuri who used to lend money at extremely high interest rates (see USURY). His customers finally caught on to Yuri, and now he's on the street, completely penniless, trying to earn food money by selling old pens. His new slogan: "Please buy from Pen Yuri. I'm broke."

Other forms: Penurious *(adj);* penuriously *(adv)*

PERFUNCTORY (per-FUNK-ter-ee) *adj* — without enthusiasm or thoroughness; routine; "going through the motions"

Looks like: perfume factory

Picture: The woman responsible for inspecting a perfume factory has just completed her tour in a little under three minutes. Her assistant, a young man in training, is amazed at how short their inspection was: "We hardly looked at anything in there. What kind of inspection is this?" Her response: "A perfunctory one. Look, why should I push myself? I've been through here a hundred times before. I never find anything, I write them a positive report, and I always come out smelling like a rose!"

Other forms: Perfunctoriness *(noun)*; perfunctorily *(adv)*

PERNICIOUS (per-NISH-uss) *adj* — destructive

Sounds like: burn his shoes

Picture: A man in a prison cell. The man's cellmate is destructive, and one day, when he comes back to the cell he finds that his shoes have been burned up.

Other forms: Perniciousness *(noun)*; perniciously *(adv)*

PERSPICACITY (per-spih-KASS-it-ee) *noun* — mental sharpness; keen insight; shrewdness

Sounds like: perspire Cassidy

Picture: Cassidy's been brought down to police headquarters for questioning. There doesn't seem to be any evidence at all against him, but as the detective asks his probing questions, he makes a shrewd observation: "You say you weren't there, but I notice you're starting to perspire, Cassidy. Is it possible you know more about this crime than you're admitting?"

Other forms: Perspicacious *(adj)*; perspicaciously *(adv)*

PERUSE (puh-ROOZ) *verb* — read carefully; study in detail

Sounds like: Peru's

Picture: A man carefully reading a giant map of Peru.

Other form: Perusal *(noun)*

PERVADE (per-VADE) *verb* — to spread to every part

Sounds like: parade

Picture: It had been raining all morning, but just as the parade began, the clouds moved away and the sun appeared. Instantly, a feeling of joy pervaded the crowd (marchers and spectators alike.)

Other forms: Pervasiveness, pervasion *(nouns)*; pervasively *(adv)*

PETULANCE (PETCH-oo-lence) *noun* — **grouchiness**

Sounds like: pet chew Lance

Picture: Lance has a dog who likes to chew on one of those fake rawhide bones. The dog chews all day and even in his sleep, and has been doing this for years. But today Lance is in a bad mood. He's not sure why, but he's cranky, and his pet is just chewing and chewing on that bone and it's getting on his nerves. Finally, Lance can't take it anymore: "Would you stop chewing on that stupid bone? All day and all night for eight years I've been listening to you chomp on that thing. I've been patient, extremely patient, I think, but I have to tell you that it's driving me absolutely crazy!"

Other forms: Petulant *(adj);* petulantly *(adv)*

PHLEGMATIC (fleg-MAT-ick) *adj* — **calm; unemotional**

Sounds like: flag medic

Picture: A medic (military doctor) holding a flag. Fireworks light up the sky behind them, but both the medic and flag remain limp.

PIOUS (PIE-us) *adj* — **exhibiting religious devotion**

Sounds like: pies

Picture: Pies praying. Or someone praying to a pie.

Other forms: Piety *(noun);* piously *(adv)*

PITHY (PITH-ee) *adj* — **to the point; concise**

Sounds like: pity

Picture: A TV news reporter stands at someone's front door. "Sir, you live next door to Mr. Jobe, whose house, as you know, was flattened by an asteroid around noon today. What you may not know is that Mr. Jobe was served with divorce papers this morning while he was at court filing for personal bankruptcy. Shorty afterward, his car was stolen while he was having emergency root canal work done, and so he has been unable to see the charred shell of his house. Would you tell our audience what you think of the kind of day Mr. Jobe has been having?" The man says simply, "Pity."

Other forms: Pith, pithiness *(nouns)*

PLACATE (PLAY-kate) *verb* — **to appease; pacify; mollify**

Sounds like: play Kate

Picture: Three girls are playing hopscotch on the sidewalk. Kate, who is younger than the others, is sitting on a nearby bench, obviously upset that she's been excluded from the game. Finally, in an effort to pacify her, one of the girls says, "It's okay, you can play, Kate." When she hears the invitation, Kate's face lights up and she happily joins the others.

Other form: Placatory *(adj)*

81

PLATITUDE (PLAT-ih-tood) *noun* — **dull, trite statement**

Sounds like: plate a tooth

Picture: A dental office. The patient is having one of his teeth plated. (Whatever that means. I don't know, maybe it doesn't mean anything. I'm not a dentist. Anyway, it doesn't matter, just pretend you know what plating is.) So he's in the chair and he has about eighteen different clamps in and around his mouth, his gums are filled with cotton balls, the little suction thing is stuck to his tongue, and he tastes blood. The dentist, meanwhile, is trying to be entertaining. But all he can come up with is one stupid, boring remark after another, like "Isn't this an experience you can sink your <u>teeth</u> into?" "I hope this doesn't take too much of a <u>bite</u> out of your bank account!" "Just relax. You won't feel any pain, just a little pressure..."

Other forms: Platitudinous *(adj)*; platitudinously *(adv)*

PLAUSIBLE (PLAWS-ih-bull) *adj* — **believable, but not completely**

Sounds like: Claus or Bill

Picture: Two little girls studying the Santa Claus who has appeared at their door. They want to believe it's really Santa Claus, and they're 95% sure it is, but there's just something about his voice that tells them it might be their neighbor, Bill. "It definitely <u>could</u> be the real Santa Claus," says one. "Well, I say we give him the benefit of the doubt," says the other. "That 'Ho Ho Ho' sounded plausible to me."

Other forms: Plausibility *(noun)*; plausibly *(adv)*

POMPOUS (POMP-us) *adj* — **filled with self-importance; arrogant; obnoxiously proud**

Sounds like: pom-poms

Picture: The new head cheerleader at the high school has just been chosen and she has decided to appear before an assembly of the entire school to tell everyone how much she deserves the honor and how lucky they are to have her. "And now," she says, waving her pom-poms over her head, "how about a big cheer for me?"

Other forms: Pomposity *(noun)*; pompously *(adv)*

PONDEROUS (PONN-der-uss) *adj* — **slow; weighty; labored**

Sounds like: pond of rust

Picture: Creatures made of metal wading through a pond. As they begin to rust, their movements become slower and more difficult.

Other form: Ponderously *(adv)*

PORTENT (POR-tent) *noun* — **warning sign; omen; indication**

Sounds like: poor tent

Picture: A wife, husband, son, and daughter on their first camping trip. The children are watching their parents try to pitch the tent. When the tent is finally up, it is small, shaky, and has several holes in it. The daughter says to her brother, "I have a feeling that poor tent is a sign of things to come this weekend."

Other forms: Portend *(verb);* portentious *(adj)*

POTENT (PO-tent) *adj* — **powerful**

Looks like: patent

Picture: Two boys in their classroom, the teacher unconscious on the floor. One boy says to the other, "Hey, we should patent that spitball. It's potent!"

Other form: Potency *(noun)*

Connect with: Potentate, potential

PRECARIOUS (pree-KAIR-ee-yuss) *adj* — **risky; uncertain**

Sounds like: please carry us

Picture: Two children following their father on a hike along the edge of a cliff. "Dad," cries one of them, "We're afraid we might fall. Please carry us."   Other forms: Precariously *(adv);* precariousness *(noun)*

PRECLUDE (pre-KLOOD) *verb* — **prevent; make impossible**

Sounds like: pre-glued

Picture: Young boy proudly showing his father a large stack of envelopes; there is a bottle of glue on the desk. "Hey, Dad, these envelopes of yours were supposed to be pre-glued but I don't think they were. So I decided to save you a lot of work by glueing them closed. Pretty smart, huh?" (Father thinks: "Well, I guess this precludes me from mailing anything in those envelopes.")

Other forms: Preclusion *(noun);* preclusive *(adj)*

PRECOCIOUS (pre-KO-shuss) *adj* — **mature at a young age**

Sounds like: pre-coat shoes

Picture: A young boy dressed in a business suit. His mother is admiring his stylish shoes. "Those are beautiful shoes, dear. Just don't forget to wear your coat." The boy's response: "Please don't talk to me as though I were a child, Mother. I am, after all, nearly eight years old."

Other forms: Precociously *(adv);* precocity *(noun)*

PREDECESSOR (PRED-ih-sess-or) *noun* — an earlier occupant of a job, office, or position

Sounds like: pretty scissor

Picture: Two servants are talking in the mansion where they work. The man is admiring the woman's scissors, which are sterling silver and have precious stones set into the handles around the finger holes. "What pretty scissors!" he says. "Yes," she responds, "they were given to me by my predecessor. She worked here as the family's coupon clipper for nearly thirty years!"

PREDILECTION (pred-ih-LEK-shun) *noun* — a preference for something

Sounds like: bread election

Picture: The judge at a bread baking contest. The different loaves are displayed on a table, but the judge is looking away, eyes closed. She knew right from the beginning which bread she would choose.

PRETENTIOUS (pre-TENCH-us) *adj* — showy; making ridiculous claims; excessively ambitious

Sounds like: pretend shoes

Picture: A man showing his new shoes to his family. He is proud of everything he does, to the point of being unrealistic. But regarding these shoes, he seems to be even more out of touch with reality than usual. He calls them his "pretend shoes," and he says that while wearing them, he'll be able to fly.

Other forms: Pretension *(nouns)*; pretentiously *(adv)*

PREVALENT (PREV-uh-lent) *adj* — widely-accepted; common; prevailing

Sounds like: provolone (a type of cheese)

Picture: You're visiting a small village in Italy. Almost immediately you notice that everywhere you go in this village, you see provolone cheese. In the shops, people are buying it; in the restaurants, people are eating it; in the streets, people are holding it. You see provolone cheese on TV and in magazines. Even the mayor's name is Dom Provolone. It is, in this small Italian town, a very common cheese.

Other forms: Prevalence *(noun)*; prevalently *(adv)*

PRIMORDIAL (pry-MOR-dee-al) *adj* — formed long ago; primitive

Sounds like: pry Morty, Al

Picture: Two archeologists have been digging in the hard soil of Turkey and have discovered the skeleton of a primitive man. As they take turns digging out "Morty," as they have nicknamed the skeleton, the archeologists cheer each other on. When Al takes his turn, his partner encourages him to pry the skeleton out from beneath a stone: "Pry him out. Pry Morty, Al. But be careful, he's very old."

Other form: Primordially *(adv)*

PRODIGAL (PROD-ih-gull) *adj* — **wasteful, especially of money; extravagant**

Sounds like: proud of gulls

Picture: Person who has spent his entire inheritance to buy a flock of seagulls. He's very proud of his purchase, not realizing that he's squandered his fortune.

Note: Don't confuse with "prodigy," a highly-talented child.

PRODIGIOUS (pro-DIJ-uss) *adj* — **very large**

Sounds like: pro dishes

Picture: Large dishes. Prodigious is often used to describe a person's enormous appetite, so you might imagine someone eating a large amount of food from very large dishes.

Other forms: Prodigiousness *(noun)*; prodigiously *(adv)*

PROFOUND (pro-FOWND) *adj* — **penetrating beyond the superficial; filled with wisdom and insight; deep**

Looks like: Prof. Found

Picture: A philosophy professor from the local college had been missing for a week, but he's been discovered alive and well, trapped at the bottom of an abandoned mine shaft. The headline in today's newspaper: "PROF FOUND!" Upon first seeing his rescuers, the professor looks up and says, "I am a symbol of mankind, fallen from the heights of power and wisdom to the depths of despair and destitution, until you, the gods of Goodness and Health, arrived to bring me the gifts of freedom and rebirth." Looking down from the top of the mine shaft, one rescuer says to the other: "Wow, that's deep!"

Other forms: Profundity *(noun)*; profoundly *(adv)*

Don't confuse with "profane," which means "vulgar" or "disrespectful of sacred things" (profanity).

PROFUSE (pro-FYOOS) *adj* — **in large amounts or quantities**

Looks like: Prof. Fuse

Picture: A physics instructor named Prof. Fuse has invited you into his office. As you enter, you notice that the room is overflowing with fuses of all kinds — car fuses, boat fuses, house fuses. Everywhere you look — on the shelves, under the desk, in the light fixtures — are hundreds of fuses. "Prof. Fuse," you say, "what a profusion of fuses!" (It's a weird thing to say, but it fits.)

Other forms: Profuseness, profusion *(noun)*; profusely *(adv)*

PROTRACT (pro-TRAKT) *verb* — **extend in time or space**

Sounds like: pro track

Picture: Young women running on a track. Eventually they notice that a crew of workmen is digging up the track in order to make it bigger. The men explain to the runners: "No more amateur stuff. This is going to be a pro track from now on, so we have to make it regulation size for professional races."

Other forms: Protraction *(noun)*; protractive *(adj)*

PROVOKE (pruh-VOKE) *verb* — **to anger; to stir up or arouse**

Sounds like: prove oak

Picture: Two women out in the forest. One points out a tree and says it's an oak. The other disagrees; she thinks it's some other kind of tree. As they walk, the first woman pulls "The Tree Handbook" out of her coat pocket, opens up to the section on oaks, and proves to her friend that the tree in question is indeed an oak. Not satisfied with being right, she then resorts to mocking and insulting her companion with comments such as: "What kind of tree did you think it was? I mean, any fool could see that was an oak from a mile away! You must be the dumbest living thing in this forest! Let me ask you this, did you know it was a tree?" The victim of this provocation grows angrier and angrier, until she cannot listen any more. She bends down, picks up a small oak log, and whacks her friend over the head with it.

Other forms: Provocative *(adj)*; provokingly *(adv)*; provocation *(noun)*

PROXIMITY (proks-IM-ih-tee) *noun* — **nearness; closeness**

Looks like: a combination of "approximate" and "vicinity." Something in the approximate vicinity is nearby.

Other forms: Proximate *(adj)*; proximately *(adv)*

PRUDENT (PROO-dent) *adj* — **wise; shrewd; cautious**

Sounds like: prune dent

Picture: Two gangs are on opposite sides of the street. They're having their monthly prune war, in which they continue to throw prunes at each other until one side gives up. Your car is parked in the street, directly in the line of fire. It's a new car, without a scratch, and you wish to keep it that way. So, to avoid prune dents and other such blemishes, you prudently run to the car and drive it to safety.

Other forms: Prudently *(adv)*; prudence *(noun)*; prudential *(adj)*

PUERILE (PYUR-ill) or (PYUR-ile) *adj* — **childish**

"Puerile" looks like a combination of "purely" and "juvenile." Juvenile means childish, so think of someone who's purely juvenile.

Other form: Puerility *(noun)*

QUALIFY (KWAL-ih-fye) *verb* — **to limit the meaning of a previous statement; to modify**

Sounds like: Wally Fly
Sounds exactly like: qualify (as in, to be suitable for a position)
Let's combine the two.

Picture: Wally Fly is a fly who screens applicants wishing to work directly for the queen. When she asks him if a certain candidate is qualified for the job, he replies, "Yes, Your Highness, I would be willing to bet my life that he is qualified... Well, maybe not my life, but I'd risk my job to say he's the right one. I take that back. I don't mean that if he doesn't work out that you should fire me. I'm just saying that he's the best applicant we've had. Well, so far, anyway. I doubt very much that we'll get a better one. But then again, a better one could come along. Who knows, really...?"

Other forms: Qualifier *(noun)*; qualified *(adj)*; qualifiedly *(adv)*

QUANDARY (KWON-dree) *noun* — **a state of confusion or doubt; dilemma**

Sounds like: coin tree

Picture: An apple tree filled with ripe apples. The tree has what appears to be a coin slot in the middle of its trunk. A woman approaches and reads a sign next to the tree: "Apples 25 cents. Please deposit correct change in slot." The woman seems to be confused and unsure what to do. She's in a quandary.

QUARANTINE (KWAR-en-teen) *noun* — **forced isolation to prevent the spread of disease**

Sounds like: car and teen

Picture: Sick teenager locked inside a car. "I can't come out for forty days?" he asks. "But really, it's just allergies!"

Other form: Quarantine *(verb)*; quarantined *(adj)*

QUELL (KWELL) *verb* — **to calm; pacify**

Looks like: a combination of 'queen' and 'quill'

Picture: A violent riot is taking place just outside the castle. The queen comes to a window, waves a quill (feather) over the crowd, and everyone immediately calms down and goes peacefully home.

QUERULOUS (KWER-uh-luss) *adj* — constantly complaining

Sounds like: squirrel louse

Picture: Squirrel loudly complaining about a louse that's biting his back. (Louse is the singular of lice.)

Note: Querulous is <u>not</u> related to the word "query," which means to question.

RAMPANT (RAMM-pent) *adj* — unrestrained; widespread

Looks like: ramp ant

Picture: Thousands of ants running up the ramp to the ark. Noah is saying, "Two! I said two!" (Looking on, one anteater says to the other: "And you were worried about the food on this cruise.")

RATIFY (RAT-ih-fy) *verb* — approve (by formal vote, for example); confirm

Sounds like: rat to fly

Picture: The pilots' union has just ratified a new agreement with the airlines. As part of the agreement, rats will now be allowed to fly commercial jets (but only if they meet the height requirement).

Other form: Ratification *(noun)*

REBUFF (ree-BUFF) *verb* — to ignore or reject strongly; snub

Looks like: re-buff

Picture: A young woman is waxing and buffing her car for the third time that day. Without even looking away from the car, she says to a young man passing by, "No, Jerry, I can't go out with you tonight. I have to re-buff my car. Quite a few more times. Try me again, maybe in October."

REBUTTAL (re-BUTT-ul) *noun* — denial or contradiction; argument; refutation

Sounds like: re-butter

Picture: Husband and wife are both judges. One evening, at the dinner table with their two children, they get into a courtroom scene about whether the butter is too hard for the bread.
    She: "This butter is just the right consistency. I submit that if you're careful about taking thin slices, Dear, it spreads quite easily on the bread."
    He: "You say the butter is the right consistency, <u>Darling</u>. But isn't it true that while I wasn't looking, you secretly ran your knife under the hot water so that it would soften the butter when you used it?"
    She: "I would like to call my first witness to the stand. Our daughter, Jennifer."
    Jennifer to her brother: "I wish we could just eat dinner like everybody else."
    Brother: "Yeah. And why do they have to wear those stupid robes every night?"

    Other form: Rebut *(verb)*

RECANT (re-CANT) *verb* — **take back something you've said; withdraw a statement or belief**

Sounds like: recount

Picture: A candidate speaking to supporters on the night of a close election: "My friends, earlier this evening, I demanded a recount of the votes. I am now recanting that request. I do <u>not</u> want a recount, and am conceding defeat. (See CONCEDE)

RECLUSE (REK-loose) *noun* — **person who prefers to be alone all the time; someone withdrawn from the rest of society**

Sounds like: wreck clues

Picture: A woman walking backward, about to enter her log cabin in the woods. As she walks, she sweeps away her footprints in the snow. "Have to wreck these clues," she says, "so no one will find me. I don't want to see <u>anyone</u>."

Other forms: Reclusive *(adj);* reclusion *(noun)*

RECONDITE (REK-un-dite) *adj* — **hidden; difficult to understand; profound**

Sounds like: reckon I

Picture: A young man has wandered into a secret corner in the basement of the public library, where he's found a large, dusty book called, "The Mysteries of Life." After reading a few pages in the book, he says, "I reckon I (recondite) don't understand what any of this means."

Other forms: Reconditeness *(noun);* reconditely *(adv)*

REDOLENT (REDD-uh-lint) *adj* — **strongly scented; fragrant**

Sounds like: red doe lint

Picture: A doe (female deer) has red lint on her back. The lint is giving off a very powerful fragrance, which has attracted a male deer. ("You scent for me?" he asks.)

Other form: Redolence *(noun)*

REDUNDANT (re-DUN-dent) *adj* — **more than what is necessary; repetition of words or ideas in speech or writing**

Sounds like: Red done that

Picture: Two little children being given a list of chores by their mother. As she reads off the list, they respond to each item by saying, "Red done that!" Red is their older brother, and he has already done everything on the list. Their mother, however, still wants them to do each chore. "But, Mom!" plead the children. "Isn't that redundant?" "Yes," she responds. "It is redundant. It's also more than what is necessary. And in speech or writing, in this case, speech, it's a repetition of words or ideas. Now go do it anyway."

Other forms: Redundancy *(noun);* redundantly *(adv)*

89

RELEGATE (RELL-uh-gate) *verb* — **reduce or demote to an inferior place or position; banish**

Sounds like: reel a gate

Picture: As head butler at the estate, he'd been in charge of a staff of thirty. But when the boss died and the young brat took over the house, he was demoted to the most meaningless and embarrassing job of all: he had to sit out on the lawn with a fishing pole. The fishing line was attached to the front gate, and when a visitor's car came up the driveway, he reeled in the gate until it opened.

Other form: Relegation *(noun)*

RELEVANCY (RELL-uh-vent-see) *noun* — **having a clear relationship to the matter at hand**

Sounds like: really fancy

Picture: A student named Germaine is answering a question about the planet Neptune, but he is bringing up things that have nothing (or very little) to do with the question: "Well, see, when they discovered the planet Neptune, the man who found it was living in this really fancy house in a really fancy town, and his wife had on this really fancy dress and they went out to celebrate at this really fancy restaurant..." The teacher finally interrupts: "Germaine, that's all very interesting but I don't think it's relevant."

Other form: Relevant *(adj)*

REMORSE (ree-MORSE) *noun* — **a feeling of guilt; regret; self-reproach**

Looks exactly like: re-Morse (as in Morse Code)

Picture: A man sending a second message to his girlfriend by Morse Code. He taps out on the telegraph that he's sorry for what he said in his first message. The dots and dashes say simply, "FEELING GUILTY. VERY SORRY. PLEASE FORGIVE."

Other forms: Remorseful *(adj)*; remorsefully *(adv)*

These "rep" words form the names of elected representatives.

REPRIMAND (REP-rih-mand) *verb* — **scold; criticize**

Sounds like: Rep. Raymond

Picture: Representative Raymond has an unusual approach to campaigning. He walks around the city scolding and criticizing the voters for their beliefs. (Read about his colleague — see REPROVE.)

REPROVE (re-PROOV) *verb* — **scold; criticize; disapprove of**

Sounds like: Rep. Prove

Picture: From the same city as Rep. Raymond, Rep. Prove takes the very same approach to campaigning: he stops people on the street, asks for their opinion, tries to prove them wrong, them criticizes them.

90   Other forms: Reproval, reproof *(nouns)*; reprovingly *(adv)*

REPUDIATE (reh-PYOOD-ee-ate) *verb* — **disown; reject**

Sounds like: Rep. Rudy Yate

Picture: Representative Rudy Yate is running for re-election. He recently announced that he would disown, reject, and positively repudiate all those gifts he received from local businesses the last time he campaigned ("If I can still find 'em, of course.")

Other form: Repudiation *(noun)*

THERE IS ONE RESERVED RESERVE.

RESERVE (ree-ZURV) *noun* — **the ability to control your emotions and actions; self-restraint**

Sounds exactly like: reserve (as in Army Reserve — a person in the Army on a part-time basis).

Picture: A private being screamed at by the sergeant. The other privates look on, amazed by their friend's ability to stay calm and unemotional as he endures his punishment.

Other form: Reserved *(adj)*

RESIGN (re-ZYNE) *verb* — **give in; acquiesce; relinquish**

Sounds exactly like: resign (as in, quit a job)

Picture: A Cabinet member is surrounded by the President, Vice President, all the other Cabinet members, and the president's staff. This particular Cabinet member is widely hated by nearly everyone in the administration, as well as much of the general public. As he looks around the room at a sea of hostile faces he says, "All right, all right, I can't fight all of you. I guess I'll have to resign."

Other forms: Resigned *(adj)*; resignation *(noun)*; resignedly *(adv)*

RESOLVE (ree-ZOLVE) *noun* — **determination; strong will**

Looks like: re-solve (solve again)

Picture: A detective has just received word that a case he solved ten years ago has been re-opened because of new evidence. The detective spent many months on the case the first time, partly because the victim was a close friend of his. He's determined to solve the case again, no matter how long it takes. "My New Year's Resolution will be to re-solve this case," he says, "and put it to rest once and for all."

Other forms: Resolved *(adj)*; resolution *(noun)*; resolve *(verb)*

Note: A New Year's Resolution is a promise that you are going to do something difficult, something that requires a great deal of determination.

RETICENT (RETT-ih-sent) *adj* — **quiet; uncommunicative**

Sounds like: redder cent

Picture: A giant penny is being painted red. The penny sits quietly as the artist repeatedly asks, "Redder, Cent. Do you want to be redder? Cent? Huh? Penny for your thoughts. Hello, Cent..."

Other forms: Reticence *(noun)*; reticently *(adv)*

NOW THERE'S SOMEONE YOU CAN LOOK UP TO.

PAUL REVERE

REVERE (ree-VEER) *verb* — **greatly respect**

Sounds exactly like: Revere (Paul Revere's last name)

Picture: Young boy and girl dwarfed by large statue of Paul Revere. They are looking at the statue with great respect.

Other form: Reverence *(noun)*

ROTUND (roe-TUND) *adj* — **round**

Looks like: round, with a T in the middle

Picture: The word ROTUND in large letters. The "T" has dropped down to serve as a pedestal for the other letters, which spell the word ROUND.

Other form: Rotundity *(noun)*

RUDIMENTARY (rood-ih-MEN-ter-ee) *adj* — **undeveloped; fundamental; elementary**

Looks like: Rudy elementary

Picture: Rudy's Elementary School, where the students learn only the simplest of concepts. In math, they never get past 2+2, in spelling, 'cat' is the most difficult word they study, and in art, they get an 'A' if they can distinguish red from yellow.

Other forms: Rudiment *(noun)*; rudimentarily *(adv)*

SALUBRIOUS (suh-LOOB-ree-uss) *adj* — **promoting health**

Looks like: Sal's Libraries

Picture: A library owned by a man named Sal. The library is filled with books and magazines, but they're all about health. Library patron: "Excuse me, sir, do you have any books on disease, sickness, or death?" Sal: "Sorry, at Sal's Libraries we only have books on health." (See SALUTARY.)

Other form: Salubrity *(noun)*

SALUTARY (SAL-yoo-terr-ee) *adj* — **promoting health, or having some beneficial effect**

Sounds like: Sal U. Terry

Picture: A traveling salesman in the 1800s. He's talking to a small crowd about "Sal U. Terry's Amazing Health & Vitality Elixir. It's guaranteed to make you feel better within one week, or you come and find me for a full refund. And if you need more information, just go down to one of Sal's Libraries and read all about this healthy concoction."

Connect with: Salubrious

Note: Don't confuse with "salutatory," which has to do with a welcome or greeting.

SANCTION (SANK-shun) *verb* — **approve; give consent**

Sounds like: sank Shawn

Picture: You're rowing a boat out on the lake. Shawn, a man you've hated for eleven years, is rowing his boat on the other side of the lake. A friend suddenly shows up in the water right next to your boat and tells you that he just sank Shawn. The friend still holds the drill he used to bore a hole in the bottom of Shawn's boat. You pause for a second, then smile and say, "Good work. I normally don't like that kind of behavior, but if you tell me you sank Shawn, I have to approve."

Opposite meaning: This is confusing, but as a noun, a 'sanction' is an action taken in order to punish or change another's behavior. For example, governments often impose economic sanctions against a nation they feel is behaving badly.

SANGUINE (SANG-gwinn) *adj* — **optimistic; cheerful**

Sounds like: sang win

Picture: A young woman is in a singing contest and has just finished her song. She comes backstage and says to her mother, "I know I won. I <u>sang</u> more than well enough to <u>win</u>. I'm sure of it!"

Other forms: Sanguineness *(noun);* sanguinely *(adv)*

SARDONIC (sar-DONN-ik) *adj* — **humorous, but humor tinged with sarcasm or disdain; cynical**

Sounds like: Sardine Nick

Picture: A sardine named Nick who's working as a stand-up comedian. Much of his act consists of sardonic, sarcastic humor.

Other form: Sardonically *(noun)*

93

SCANTY (SCANT-ee) *adj* — small in quantity; insufficient

Looks like: scan tea

Picture: The lady named Emma who gives tea to anyone who comes by (see AMITY). One day, with a few hundred people waiting at her front door, Emma goes to the pantry to get more teabags. She typically has dozens of boxes, but as she scans the tea on the shelves, she realizes that she has very little — certainly not enough for such a large number of uninvited guests. "Oh, dear," she says to herself, "I wonder if any of them drink coffee."

Other forms: Scantily *(adv)*; scantiness *(noun)*; scant *(adj)*

SCRUPULOUS (SKROOP-yoo-luss) *adj* — very thorough; or, doing what is right and ethical

Sounds like: scoop you loose

Picture: You're lying on the beach, enjoying the last rays of warm sunshine. Everyone else has left, so the beach is deserted except for you and your radio. Out of the corner of your eye, you see a gang of five-year-old children approaching your blanket. There are perhaps nine or ten of them, each armed with a plastic pail and shovel. Several are wearing necklaces made out of what appear to be shark's teeth. You grow a little uneasy, but remind yourself that they're only children. The next thing you know, you've been yanked out of your chair, your hands and feet tied, and you're being buried standing up about ten feet from the water's edge. Five minutes later, up to your lower lip in sand, you watch the gang of children walk off down the beach. You attempt to squirm free but can't move. You check the angle of the sun and try to estimate how much time you have before high tide. As apprehension slowly turns to panic, you notice that one of the children has returned, plastic shovel in hand. "What are you going to do?" you ask nervously. "I'm going to scoop you loose," he answers. "It's the only ethical thing to do." And he begins to dig you out of the sand, carefully, methodically, one tiny scoop at a time.

Other forms: Scrupulousness *(noun)*; scrupulously *(adv)*

SCRUTINIZE (SKROO-tin-ize) *verb* — examine closely; inspect carefully

Sounds like: screwed-in eyes

Picture: A "Frankenstein's Monster Look-Alike Contest." The judge is holding a magnifying glass and examining one of several monsters lined up for inspection. "Hmmm," says the judge. "Screwed-in eyes. Minus five points. The eyes should be plug-ins."

Other form: Scrutiny *(noun)*

SECLUSION (seh-KLOO-zhun) *noun* — separation from other people; isolation

Sounds like: sick Lucien

Picture: Two people standing outside a closed door. One says to the other, "Lucien is sick and wants to be left alone."

Other form: Secluded *(adj)*

SECTARIAN (sek-TAIR-ee-un) *adj* — limited to the beliefs of a small group, such as a religious sect; narrow in scope

Sounds like: secretary Ann

Picture: A secretary, Ann, who belongs to a religious group consisting of other secretaries. On her coffee break, she preaches to co-workers: "I'm not interested in ritual. I'm interested in the religion of secretaries. What kind of correction fluid will lead us to freedom from the bondage of retyping? Where are we to find ultimate truth, in the dictionary or in the spell checker? Is there an afterlife, and if so, what color Post-It Notes do they use there?"

Other form: Sect *(noun)*

SEDITIOUS (seh-DISH-uss) *adj* — trying to stir up a revolt against an authority figure

Sounds like: said dishes

Picture: The mother is telling her son, for the fourth time, to please wash the dishes ("I said <u>dishes</u>!") But the son is being urged by his older sister to refuse: "Tell her you won't do it. If you wash them tonight, she'll just tell you to do them again next week."

Other forms: Sedition *(noun)*; seditiously *(adv)*

SENTENTIOUS (sen-TENN-shuss) *adj* — short and to the point; terse

Sounds like: send ten shoes

Picture: Mother and father reading a very short letter from their daughter, who is away studying dance. It says, "Love dance school. Send ten shoes."

Other forms: Sententiousness *(noun)*; sententiously *(adv)*

SERPENTINE (SIR-pen-tine) *adj* — coiled; twisted; winding

Looks like: serpent
Rhymes with: Turpentine

Picture: A serpent (snake) that has coiled itself around a can of turpentine. The curved shape of the snake's body would be described as serpentine.

SERVILE (SERV-ile) *adj* — like a slave; subservient; submissive

Sounds like: serve aisle

Picture: A man in a movie theater. He gets up to get popcorn, not for himself or his date, but for everyone in their aisle. He buys the snacks and serves them, all the time apologizing for being so slow and inconsiderate.

Other form: Servility *(noun)*

95

SKEPTIC (SKEP-tik) *noun* — **one who doesn't believe unless he's shown absolute proof; doubter**

Sounds like: skip tick

Picture: A man is in a museum looking at the world's most accurate watch, housed in a display case. According to the sign, the watch will lose less than a second every million years. The man compares the ticking of this magnificent timepiece with the watch he's wearing on his arm. To his surprise, he finds that the museum watch skips a tick every time the second hand goes around. In other words, it loses a second every minute! He runs to tell the museum director, but the director refuses to believe the story. "Impossible," he says. "That's the most accurate watch ever made. Skipped a tick? I refuse to believe it."

Other forms: Skepticism *(noun)*; skeptical *(adj)*; skeptically *(adv)*

SLANDER (SLAN-der) *noun* — **negative oral remarks about another person that are untrue**

Sounds like: slammed her

Picture: Couple watching television talk show. Referring to female guest on the show, one of the viewers says, "Boy she really slammed her! 'Liar. Thief. Killer.' And to think she was talking about her own mother!"

Other forms: Slander *(verb)*; slanderous *(adj)*

SLOUGH (SLUFF) *verb* — **discard; cast off; shed**

Rhymes with: stuff

Picture: The "Slough and Stuff Clinic," where snakes go to donate their old skin (which they slough off). Other less fortunate snakes come by to be matched up with the old skins and then stuffed into them. (Says one of the sloughers on his way out: "Hey, if the dinosaurs had recycled, who knows?")

SOLEMN (SOL-im) *adj* — **serious; somber; grave**

Sounds like: sell 'em

Picture: They used to be wealthy, but no more. They've spent their savings, sold their cars, and rented out their house. Now they're gathering some of their possessions for a tag sale to raise money for food. When the woman holds up her husband's golf clubs, his face sags into a serious expression and he says sadly, "Sell 'em."

Other forms: Solemnity *(noun)*; solemnly *(adv)*

SOMBER (SOMM-ber) *adj* — **dark; gloomy**

Looks like: sombrero (Mexican hat)

Picture: A village in Mexico, where happiness and fun are not allowed. Whenever a stranger or visiting family arrives on vacation, the people of the town take out their Somber Sombreros. These magical hats instantly bring forth clouds to cover the sun, and sad feelings to drive away the joy — and the visitors.

Other forms: Somberness *(noun)*; somberly *(adv)*

SONOROUS (SAHN-er-uss) *adj* — loud, full in sound; booming

Sounds like: son of Russ

Picture: The same Russ who yells at everyone who works for him (see ONEROUS). Now Russ and his wife have a baby, a boy named Son of Russ, whose voice is unbelievably loud. Russ is on the couch trying to take a nap (Son of Russ kept him up all night). But once again, the baby's booming cry is bounding down the stairs and bouncing off the walls, right into his father's ears.

Other forms: Sonorousness *(noun)*; sonorously *(adv)*

SPECIOUS (SPEE-shuss) *adj* — having a false or misleading appearance; seemingly true, but actually false

Sounds like: spy shoes

Picture: A spy's apartment. When the enemy spy enters, he doesn't realize the shoes on the floor are really a tape recorder and video camera. They appear to be an ordinary pair of shoes.

Other forms: Speciously*(adv)*; speciousness *(noun)*

SPORADIC (spor-ADDIK) *adj* — occurring infrequently and without predictability; occasional

Sounds like: store addict

Picture: A man who is addicted to shopping. He goes to every store he can get to, browsing quickly, sometimes buying, then running out to the next store. (Observer: "Does he come in here often?" Store owner: "Nah. It's sporadic. He has a lot of stores to cover.")

Other form: Sporadically *(adv)*

SPURIOUS (SPYER-ee-us) *adj* — false; fake; misleading

Looks like: spur furious

Picture: A cowboy is furious about the spurs he just received from a mail order company. The spurs, advertised as "genuine silver-plated iron ," turned out to be made of aluminum foil. "I'm furious about these spurs," he says. "These are fake and this is false advertising." Then, after a few seconds he adds, "I'd challenge those mail order people to a showdown, but these impressive-lookin' guns they sold me are made out of cardboard."

Other forms: Spuriously *(adv)*; spuriousness *(noun)*

STAGNANT (STAG-nent) *adj* — motionless; unchanging; dull

Looks like: stage ant

Picture: An ant performing on stage. The ants in the audience begin to complain that the actor hasn't moved or said anything for an hour. Says one: "The play is starting to stagnate."

Other forms: Stagnate *(verb)*; stagnation *(noun)*

STATIC (STAT-ik) *adj* — **unchanging; motionless**

Sounds exactly like: static, as in electrical interference

Picture: A woman comes home from work, picks up the telephone, and realizes that the static she'd complained about that morning is still there. "I called the telephone company and they said they were going to get rid of this static. But nothing has changed. The static is still here." (Her son: "Maybe they couldn't understand what you were saying with all that static.")

Other forms: Stasis *(noun);* statically *(adv)*

STEALTH (STELTH) *noun* — **secretive behavior**

Looks like: steal wealth

Picture: A very quiet, highly-skilled burglar breaking into the home of a wealthy person. Everything the burglar does (or doesn't do) in getting into the house without being detected is an example of stealth.

Other forms: Stealthy *(adj);* stealthily *(adv)*

STOIC (STO-ik) *noun* — **a person who shows no response to pleasure or pain; someone who is impassive**

Sounds like: his toe wick

Picture: A man who makes candles by pouring melted wax over his foot. After the wax hardens, he lights his big toe, which acts as the wick. Even with his toe wick burning, the man shows no sign of pain!

Other forms: Stoic, stoical *(adj);* stoically *(adv)*

STYMIE (STY-mee) *verb* — **block; get in the way of; hamper**

Sounds exactly like: Stymie (remember the character on "The Little Rascals"?)

Note: "Stymie" originally referred to a golf situation in which one ball blocked another on the green.

Picture: Stymie (the little boy) playing golf against a professional golfer. Both players have reached the green, and as his opponent is about to putt, Stymie jumps up and runs onto the green between the hole and the other player. "I'm going to block his shot," he says, "or my name isn't Stymie!"

Other forms: Stymie *(noun);* stymied *(adj)*

SUBJUGATE (SUB-juh-gate) *verb* — **take over; enslave**

Sounds like: sub jug gate

Picture: Pirates who have switched from ferries (see NEFARIOUS) to submarines. They take over the sub by knocking the crew unconscious with jugs and gates. Then they use the crew as slave labor.

Other form: Subjugation *(noun)*

SUBLIME (suh-BLIME) *adj* — **of very special quality; noble**

Looks like: sub lime

Picture: A sub (submarine) shaped like a lime. This sub is so wonderful that it floats in the air above the water.

Other form: Sublimely *(adv)*

SUBTLE (SUT-il) *adj* — **hard to see or understand; elusive**

Looks like : subtitle

Picture: Man and woman watching a foreign film. As each subtitle appears on the screen, the audience laughs longer and louder. "What?" asks the man. "What's so funny? I just don't get it." Woman: "I think these subtitles are a little too subtle for us."

Other forms: Subtly *(adv);* subtlety *(noun)*

SUCCINCT (suk-SINKT) *adj* — **short and to the point; concise**

Sounds like : suck sink

Picture: Two teenage boys are standing in the kitchen. One has his face in the sink and he's sucking up gallons of water. His friend turns and explains succinctly to his mother: "Thirsty."

Other forms: Succinctly *(adv);* succinctness *(noun)*

SUCCOR (SOOK-er) *noun*
— **help; assistance; relief**

Rhymes with: sugar

Picture: A lady's cat is stuck in a tree. A van pulls up and a bag of sugar comes to the rescue.

Other form: Succor *(verb)*

SUMPTUOUS (SUMP-choo-uss) *adj*
— **rich; magnificent**

Sounds like: some chew us

Picture: A bountiful feast set on a magnificent table. The platters rest on a linen tablecloth. The glasses are expensive crystal, the forks and spoons fine silver. Each plate of food is beautifully prepared and presented. As you approach the feast, you overhear one of the dinner rolls say to a carrot, "People are so impressed when they see us. Some chew us, but most just stand and stare!"

Other forms: Sumptuously *(adv);* sumptuousness *(noun)*

SUPERFLUOUS (soo-PURR-floo-us) *adj* — **unnecessary; extra**

Sounds like: super floss

Picture: A dental floss that's advertised as "Super Floss," so strong that one strand can lift a fleet of dump trucks without breaking. Such strength, and such claims, would be superfluous — unnecessary, far beyond the possible needs of any customer.

Other forms: Superfluously *(adv);* superfluity *(noun)*

SURREPTITIOUS (sir-rupp-TISH-uss) *adj* — **secret**

Sounds like: syrup tissues

Picture: A spy for a competitive pharmaceutical company has stolen the secret formula for "Coffee Cough Syrup," and is smuggling it out of the building in a box of tissues. (Their slogan, is: "Coffee Cough Syrup, the only cough medicine that keeps you awake while it lets your family get some sleep.")

Other form: Surreptitiously *(adv)*

SUSTAIN (suh-STANE) *verb* — **support; nurture; take on**

Looks like: Sue Stain

Picture: Sue Stain is the best stain remover in town. Everyone calls Sue whenever they have a stain they can't get out, because she does so much more than just remove stains. Sue offers emotional support, sustaining the family through the ordeal. She provides physical strength, as well, often sustaining the weight of a car while cleaning an oil stain on the driveway. Sue Stain has sustained many injuries while doing her job, yet she has somehow sustained a love for her work.

Other forms: Sustenance *(noun);* sustaining, sustainable *(adj)*

SYCOPHANT (SIK-oh-fant) *noun* — **someone who flatters in order to gain favor; wimpy follower**

Sounds like: sicko fan

Picture: There's this rock star. She is incredibly successful, with hit records coming out every week. She also seems to have more and more fans who follow her wherever she goes. One is the president of her fan club. He writes her letters of praise every day, constantly tells her she's the greatest musician in history, and has even begun to dress like her so that she will like him. But while she appreciates the attention to some degree, she doesn't like or respect this person, and often describes him as "that sicko fan."

SYMMETRY (SIMM-uh-tree) *noun* — **balance; having a similar appearance on all sides**

Sounds like: similar tree

Picture: A perfect tree, absolutely balanced and in proportion on all sides. For every branch on the left side of the tree, there is a branch of the same length and in the same position on the right side.

Other form: Symmetrical *(adj)*

TACITURN (TASS-it-turn) *adj* — **quiet**

Sounds like: that's Saturn

Picture: The planet Saturn with a face. The rings are across the mouth, so it can't talk.

Other forms: Tacit *(adj);* tacitly *(adv);* taciturnity *(noun)*

Alternate approach: "Taciturnity" sounds like "tax attorney." You might picture a tax attorney working with some clients. No matter what they say, he remains quiet.

TANGENT (TAN-jint) *noun* — **a line that touches a curve at just one point; or, a comment that is off the main topic**

Sounds like: tan gent

Picture: In the winter, the sun's rays are less direct as they approach the earth (in the Northern Hemisphere). Try to imagine the rays as a single straight line and the earth as a curve. Picture those rays just glancing off the earth's surface, meeting the curve at a single point. The rays would be tangent to the earth. That's the first definition. Now let's combine that with the second definition. Picture a man with a deep tan (tan gent) standing on the beach in the middle of winter. You ask him how he got such a tan in the winter, and whether he's been using tanning lotion or going to a tanning salon. He barely addresses your question. Instead of answering, he talks about the angle of the sun's rays and explains that if you prop yourself up just the right way, you can still get a good tan in the winter.

Other forms: Tangential, tangent *(adj)*

TANTAMOUNT (TANT-uh-mount) *adj* — **equal; comparable**

Looks like: Tonto mount

Picture: As the Lone Ranger looks on, Tonto mounts his horse by jumping straight up from a standing position. The Lone Ranger is amazed: "Tonto, that mount of yours is tantamount to a ten-foot high jump at the Olympics. You could win a gold medal!" Tonto: "Only one problem. I'd need my horse to stand under the bar."

TEMPER (TEM-per) *verb* — **bring into balance; moderate**

Sounds exactly like: temper (as in, he has a bad temper)

Picture: An inventor has created a machine that will moderate a person's temper. The angry subject sits next to a panel and places a helmet on his head. The helmet's wires are attached to the panel, and as the inventor adjusts the various dials, the participant's mood begins to change; he calms down, becoming more even-tempered.

Other forms: Temper, temperance *(noun);* tempered *(adj)*

TENACIOUS (ten-AY-shuss) *adj* — **strong; persistent; determined to hold on**

Sounds like: tennis shoes

Picture: The women's finals at Wimbledon. After the match, the winner sits down to take off her tennis shoes, but she can't. Even with the help of her opponent, the judge, two ball boys, and seventeen spectators pulling at her shoes, they won't come off her feet. (Tennis shoes can be tenacious.)

Other forms: Tenacity *(noun);* tenaciously *(adv)*

TENTATIVE (TEN-ta-tiv) *adj* — **not fully developed or definitely planned; provisional**

Sounds like: tend to give

Picture: Woman interviewing a man for a job. She is responding to his question about vacation time by saying, "We tend to give two weeks' vacation the first year, but that isn't definite yet for this particular job. I'd have to let you know later."

Other forms: Tentatively *(adv);* tentativeness *(noun)*

TENUOUS (TEN-yoo-uss) *adj* — **thin; flimsy**

Sounds like: ten U.S.

Picture: You're traveling in a country where money is made of neither metal nor paper, but slabs of stone. A native of the country is showing you how his currency is so much more durable than American money. For example, his "ten pound" bill is a 12-inch x 12-inch sheet of slate that actually weighs ten pounds. "In comparison," he says, holding up a paper-thin American ten dollar bill, "this is ten U.S. Pretty thin and flimsy, wouldn't you agree?"

Other forms: Tenuousness *(noun);* tenuously *(adv)*

TERSE (TERSE) *adj* — **of few words; to the point; pithy**

Rhymes with: purse
Sounds like: t'sers (a short, concise way of saying, "it's hers")

Picture: A man is walking down the aisle of an airplane, headed for the bathroom. On the way, he trips over a purse, falls headfirst onto someone's lap, and lands face-down in a plate of food he can't recognize even that close. When he manages to pull himself back to a standing position, he's furious. Glaring at the woman seated next to the purse, the man is about to launch into a diatribe when she looks up from her magazine, gestures to the lady across the aisle, and says simply, "T'sers."

Other forms: Terseness *(noun);* tersely *(adv)*

THRIFTY (THRIF-tee) *adj* — **careful about managing money**

Rhymes with: fifty

Picture: A little boy holding a fifty dollar bill and talking to a little girl. "See this fifty?" he asks her. "I've had this since my seventh birthday. Got it from my Uncle Phil. Haven't spent a penny of it in two years. Wanna know why? It's because I'm thrifty. I keep my expenses down. I let my parents pay for my meals, my clothes, and my entertainment. And they don't charge me rent, so I have no overhead. These are tough times. You have to be careful."

Other forms: Thriftiness *(noun)*; thriftily *(adv)*

TIMOROUS (TIM-er-uss) *adj* — **afraid**

Sounds like: Tim or us

Picture: Group of teenagers outside a large, spooky house. Their friend, Tim, has somehow gotten trapped inside and now they must make a decision about going in to rescue him. "Look," says one frightened boy, "I don't see why we should go in. I think there's a ghost in this house and he's definitely going to get somebody. It's either Tim or us." "Yeah," agrees one of the girls. "Let it be Tim."

Other forms: Timorousness *(noun)*; timorously *(adv)*

Connect with: Timid. But don't confuse "timorous" with "temerity," which means "recklessness."

TIRADE (TY-rade) *noun* — **a long and bitter speech; diatribe**

Sounds like: tie raid

Picture: A man goes to his closet to get his blue tie. It isn't there. He looks for his red tie, the one with the little penguins on it. Gone. He searches for his green and white New York Jets tie. It's missing, too. In fact, there isn't a tie to be found. He storms up to his teenage son's room, flings open the boy's closet door, and finds all of his ties, hanging on a wooden rack. He then launches into a harsh, angry, biting, twenty minute speech about his son's lack of consideration. (Son, after his father has finished: "Does this mean I can't borrow your black sweater tonight?")

TORPID (TOR-pid) *adj* — **sluggish; dull; lacking enthusiasm**

Looks like: torpedo

Picture: A torpedo that was launched from a submarine has been traveling for hundreds of miles under the water. It gradually slows down and eventually comes to rest on the ocean floor, exhausted from its long trip. A curious dolphin swims over to see what's going on. "I'm just too tired," says the torpedo. "I can't even remember where I'm supposed to go or what I'm looking for. I think I'm a heat-seeking missile, but with these allergies, who can seek anything? I just want to take a nap."

Other forms: Torpor, torpidity *(nouns)*; torpidly *(adv)*

Note: Insipid, torpid, and vapid all end with "pid" and share the quality of dullness. When you see or hear one, think of the other two. It will help you remember their meanings.

TRANSLUCENT (tranz-LOO-sent) *adj* — **permitting light to pass through**

Sounds like: trains loosened

Picture: Two train cars have uncoupled (loosened). When they move apart, the sun shines between them.

Other forms: Translucence *(noun)*; translucently *(adv)*

TREPIDATION (trep-ih-DAY-shun) *noun* — **fear**

Sounds like: trap a dachshund (a dachshund is a dog with a long body and short legs)

Picture: Several young boys have set a trap for a neighborhood animal. They don't care what they catch, as long as it's breathing and they can tease it before they let it go. Waiting behind a large tree and eating salt-free pretzels, the boys hold the end of a rope whose far end is tied in a noose and hung over a branch. After several anxious minutes, a dachshund that has gotten loose from his yard walks right into the trap and the boys yank him upside down with a sudden and fierce jerk on the rope. Whooping and slapping each other on the back, the young hunters celebrate their achievement. But when they finally turn to begin torturing their victim, the look of terror in his eyes freezes their hands and feet. They are filled with guilt and regret at what they've done to this frightened dog. Carefully lowering him from the tree, they pet and hug him and feed him the last of their salt-free pretzels.

TRITE (TRITE) *adj* — **overused; common; stale**

Sounds like: trout

Picture: A trout as the teacher in a 'school' of fish. The students are bored with their teacher's constant use of cliches (dull sayings): "Remember, class, there are plenty of other fish in the sea. It's a great big ocean out there. It's sink or swim..."

Other forms: Tritely *(adv)*; triteness *(noun)*

TRUCULENT (TRUK-yoo-lent) *adj* — **aggressive; savage; cruel**

Sounds like: truck you lent

Picture: Two men fleeing from a dump truck that's about to run them down. One of the men lent the truck to the cruel driver.

Other form: Truculence *(noun)*

TURBULENCE (TUR-byoo-lence) *noun* — **violent disturbance**

Sounds like: terrible ants

Picture: Enormous ants attack a city. They squash buildings, eat entire Burger Kings, and grab airplanes out of the sky.

Other form: Turbulent *(adj)*

TYRANNY (TEER-uh-nee) *noun* — government based on absolute power or cruelty

Looks like: Tyrannosaur (the ferocious dinosaur)

Picture: A Tyrannosaurus Rex, or any mean-looking dinosaur, seated on a throne. "I am the king!" he growls. "I rule everyone! And anybody who doubts that is going to find himself extinct!"

Other form: Tyrant *(noun);* tyrannical *(adj)*

UBIQUITOUS (yoo-BIK-wit-uss) *adj* — existing everywhere at the same time

Sounds like: a Bic with us

Picture: You're orbiting the Earth in the space shuttle. As you fly over each country, you see millions of people waving their hands in the air. You look more closely and see that every person is holding a Bic cigarette lighter. Then the President calls you on the telephone to explain: "We wanted you to see at least a thousand points of light everywhere you go, so we all have a Bic with us."

Other forms: Ubiquity, ubiquitousness *(nouns);* ubiquitously *(adv)*

UNANIMOUS (yoo-NAN-ih-muss) *adj* — in total agreement

Sounds like: you, Nanny Moose

Picture: Nanny Moose (see MAGNANIMOUS) is running for president of the PTA. Immediately after the election, the members stand up and announce, "We all voted for you, Nanny Moose!"

Other forms: Unanimously *(adv);* unanimity *(noun)*

Note: "Un" means "one" and "animous" means "mind or soul." So unanimous means "of one mind."

UNDERMINE (UNN-der-mine) *verb* — to weaken by wearing away the foundation; to sabotage

Looks exactly like: under mine

Picture: A diamond mine, discovered and developed by a very hard-working woman. Secretly, the woman's jealous sister has been digging a tunnel under the mine in an effort to weaken its foundation and destroy the whole operation.

UNDULATE (UN-joo-late) *verb* — move in a wavy manner

Sounds like: under lake

Picture: The Loch Ness monster, or some other sea serpent, moving quietly through the dark waters under the lake. Seen from the side, the monster's body moves in waves under the water.

Other forms: Undulated *(adj);* undulation *(noun)*

UNERRING (un-EHR-ing) *adj* — **without making a mistake**

Sounds like: an earring

Picture: A woman wearing a pair of very beautiful earrings. Two other women look at her and one says to the other, "She never fails to wear the right earrings."

Other form: Unerringly *(adv)*

UNIFORM (YOON-ih-form) *adj* — **similar; consistent**

Sounds exactly like: uniform

Picture: A Girl Scout troop marching in a parade. One girl says, "Look at us. We're all dressed alike. Same skirts, same socks, same hats..." The other girl responds, "That's why they call them 'uniforms.'"

Other forms: Uniformity *(noun)*; uniformly *(adv)*

UNKEMPT (un-KEMPT) *adj* — **messy; sloppy**

Sounds like: encamped, or in camp

Picture: Two girls at a camp-out, seated in front of their tent. Their clothes are rumpled and dirty, their hair is uncombed.

UNPRECEDENTED (un-PRESS-ih-dent-ed) *adj* — **the first of its kind**

Sounds like: un-presidented

Picture: George Washington's inauguration. It was an unprecedented event, because he was the first.

Connect with: Precede *(verb)*. Think of "legal precedent."

UPBRAID (up-BRADE) *verb* — **criticize severely; scold**

Looks like: up braid

Picture: A schoolgirl with braided hair. She's being scolded so harshly by her teacher that her braids are standing straight up.

USURP (yoo-SERP) *verb* — **to seize or take over by force**

Sounds like: you slurp

Picture: Two women seated at the counter in a diner. One woman is slurping her soup. The other woman grabs the spoon from her and says, "You slurp and I take your spoon!"

106   Other form: Usurpation *(noun)*

USURY (YOO-zhur-ee) *noun* — **the practice of charging a very high rate of interest on loans**

Sounds like: Use Yuri. Also sounds like "usually."

Picture: A man named Yuri who lends money at high interest rates. His slogan is, "If you can afford the highest rates, Use Yuri. Otherwise, get lost." A customer reading his loan contract asks Yuri, "Do you always charge 40% interest?" Yuri answers, "Usually."

Other forms: Usurious *(adj);* usuriously *(adv)*

VACILLATE (VASS-ill-ate) *verb* — **move back and forth between choices, unable to decide**

Sounds like: vessel late

Picture: Christopher Columbus trying to decide whether to turn left or right on his way to the new world. "Go left," he says. "No, wait. Turn right. No, left..." (One of his crew says: "Chris, no pressure, but your indecision is making this vessel late, and we promised the Queen we'd get there by 1492.")

Other form: Vacillation *(noun)*

VACUOUS (VAK-yoo-us) *adj* — **empty; stupid; purposeless**

Sounds like: vacuum us

Picture: A woman is vacuuming her large living room. Over in one corner of the room sit three bathtubs (her husband collects them). They're empty, stupid, and have no real purpose. But over the sound of the machine she can hear all three of the bathtubs yelling, "Over here! Please! Vacuum us!"

Other forms: Vacuousness, vacuity *(nouns);* vacuously *(adv)*

VAGRANT (VAY-grent) *noun* — **homeless person; wanderer**

Looks like: VA Grant (VA is the abbreviation for Virginia)

Picture: A man named Grant, wearing tattered clothes and carrying his belongings in a plastic bag, answers a policeman's questions about his current residence:

"So your name is Grant?"
"Yes, sir, Officer."
"Where do you live, Mr. Grant?"
"In VA."
"VA?"
"Virginia. They call me VA Grant. My home is Virginia."
"Any particular place in Virginia?"
"Nope. It's a big state and I use all of it."

Other forms: Vagrant *(adj);* vagrantly *(adv);* vagrancy *(noun)*

VALEDICTORY (val-uh-DIK-ter-ee) *noun* — **a farewell speech**

Related to: valedictorian (the person with the highest average in a graduating class)

Picture: A high school graduating class. The valedictorian is giving her speech: "My fellow students," she says. "Goodbye. Also, farewell. See ya. Until we meet again. Bye bye. So long..." (One student to another: "I hate long goodbyes.")

Other forms: Valediction, valedictorian *(nouns)*

VALIDATE (VAL-ih-date) *verb* — **confirm; corroborate; support; sanction**

Sounds like: valid date

Picture: Two archeologists. One is handing the other a small statue and saying, "I've done all the tests on this piece and believe it was made in 1962 B.C. It was a Tuesday, July 18th. Will you please confirm that this is a valid date?"

Other forms: Valid *(adj);* validity, validation *(nouns)*

VAPID (VAH-pid) *adj* — **dull; boring; lacking flavor or spark**

Looks like: vapor

Picture: A woman is visiting a country called Vaporland. She sits with a group of boring natives as they explain their culture to her. "You see," says the leader, "everything here centers around vapor. We eat and drink only vapor. Our artwork depicts only vapor. We talk and think only about vapor. And the more dull the vapor, the more wonderful it makes us feel."

Other forms: Vapidity, vapidness *(nouns);* vapidly *(adv)*

VERACITY (ver-RASS-sih-tee) *noun* — **truth**

Looks like: Vera City

Picture: Vera City, where everyone tells the truth.

Other form: Veracious *(adj)*

Connect with: Verify

VERBOSE (ver-BOSE) *adj* — **very talkative; loquacious**

Sounds like: verb hose

Picture: A man watering his flowers with a garden hose. A steady stream of words is coming from his mouth, and from the hose!

Other forms: Verboseness, verbosity *(nouns)*

VERSATILE (VERS-uh-tile) *adj* — **having many talents or uses,**

Sounds like: reverse a tile

Picture: A TV commercial promoting Revers-a-Tile, "the amazing new floor tile with 1001 uses. Each Revers-a-Tile is a ceramic tile. Flip it over and it's a square of carpet. Flip it again and it's a square of artificial grass. Revers-a-Tile covers floors, walls, counter tops, ceilings, and driveways. It's also great for quilts, bathtubs, roofs, and highway overpasses."

Other form: Versatility *(noun)*

VESTIGE (VESS-tij) *noun* — **something left behind; a visible trace or evidence of something that has vanished**

Sounds like: vest itch

Picture: A man suffering from the itch left behind by his wool vest.

Other form: Vestigial *(adj)*

Note: Vestige is often used to refer to minor organs in the human body whose functions are not known.

VILIFY (VILL-ih-fie) *verb* — **defame; attack someone's reputation**

Sounds like: village fly

Picture: A giant fly, known as the Village Fly, who goes from house to house, saying bad things about the neighbors.

Other form: Vilification *(noun)*

VIRULENT (VEER-uh-lent) *adj* — **poisonous or destructive; filled with hate or anger; harsh**

Sounds like: Vera lint

Picture: Vera is filled with hate. So poisonous is her personality that even the lint from her clothing causes people to get sick.

Other forms: Virulence *(noun)*; virulently *(adv)*

VISCOUS (VISS-kuss) *adj* — **resistant to flow, like a very thick liquid; or, sticky**

Sounds like: biscuits

This is a somewhat confusing word, with two different meanings. But here's a way to remember both of them. Picture a pipe filled with biscuits that are half-baked. The biscuits are really a thick, sticky batter that doesn't flow through the pipe very well.

Other form: Viscosity *(noun)*. Think of motor oil.

VOLATILE (VAHL-ah-till) *adj*
— **capable of evaporating, exploding, or changing moods very quickly**

Sounds like: volley tile

Picture: A game similar to volleyball, except that instead of a ball, a tile is hit back and forth over the net. The tile is volatile and could explode at any time, so the players try to keep it in the air.

Other form: Volatility *(noun)*

VOLUBLE (VOL-yoo-bull) *adj* — **comfortable with speech; always ready to talk**

Sounds like: valuable

Picture: A glass case, filled with valuables, in a jewelry store late at night. The diamond pendant never stops talking. A watch says to a friendship ring nearby, "There she goes again! Doesn't she ever get tired? If I could just get my hands on a choker..."

Other forms: Volubility *(noun);* volubly *(adv)*

WAIVE (WAVE) *verb* — **to voluntarily abandon a legal right or privilege; relinquish; postpone**

Sounds exactly like: wave

Picture: Policeman saying, "You have the right to remain silent. If you wish to give up that right, wave your hand and start talking."

Other form: Waiver *(noun)*

WANE (WAIN) *verb* — **grow gradually smaller**

Sounds like: the name "Wayne"

Picture: Wayne is getting shorter, and his clothes are becoming too big for him.

Connect with: Wax *(verb)*

WANTON (WAHN-tun) *adj* — **excessive; uncontrolled; lustful**

Looks like: wonton (as in wonton soup)

Picture: The groom at the wedding has eaten too much wonton soup (it makes him behave as if he were drunk). Now he's wearing his bride's veil and dancing with three women at the same time. (His wife: "I knew we should've gone with the egg drop soup.")

Other forms: Wantonness *(noun);* wantonly *(adv)*

WARRANTED (WAR-ent-ed) *adj* — **justified; authorized**

Looks like: Warren Ted

Picture: Warren Ted is the town bully. He's just punched a smaller man in the nose and is walking away. The victim, lying on the ground and holding his face, says to the woman with him, "That wasn't warranted." The woman looks over at Warren Ted and says, "Yes it was. I'd recognize him anywhere."

Other forms: Warrant *(noun);* warrant *(verb)*

WASTREL (WASE-tril) *noun* — **person who wastes his money or resources**

Sounds like: waste trail

Picture: A man who has put all of his money into a backpack and set out to hike across the country. Somewhere in the woods, his money begins to fall from the backpack. As he continues to walk, unaware of the problem, he leaves behind a trail of wasted money. (Says one chipmunk to another: "He's just a wastrel on the Waste Trail of life.")

WAX (WACKS) *verb* — **grow gradually larger**

Sounds exactly like: wax

Picture: Wayne (see WANE) standing next to a ball of wax that seems to be getting larger.

Connect with: Wane *(verb).* The moon waxes (gets larger) and wanes (gets smaller) over the course of one month.

WITHER (WIH-ther) *verb* — **dry out; shrivel up; lose life or energy**

Sounds like: with her

Picture: A woman who carries old, shriveled flowers <u>with her</u> wherever she goes.

Other form: Withered *(adj)*

WIZENED (WIZZ-ind) *adj* — **old and wrinkled; withered**

Sounds like: Wiz end

Picture: The Wizard of Oz as a very, very old man (near the end of his life). He looks wrinkled and withered (but he still has enough strength and energy left to sing "If I Only Had Some Teeth").

111

XENOPHOBIA (ZEN-uh-foe-bee-uh) *noun* — **the fear or hatred of anything foreign**

Picture: A crowd of Earthlings running in fear from an alien creature and his spaceship. "Run!" they scream. "He's from the planet Xenon!"

Other form: Xenophobic *(adj)*

YIELD (YEELD) *verb* — **give up; give in**

Sounds exactly like: yield

Think of: A yield sign. When you come to a yield sign, you give in to the other driver; you surrender the right of way. So picture a man holding a yield sign and giving it to the woman standing next to him.

YOKE (YOKE) *verb* — **to link, or join together; marry**

Sounds exactly like: yolk

Picture: Two chicken farmers getting married. The man takes out a ring made of egg yolk and slides it on the woman's finger. "Now," he says, "we are yoked together forever."

Other form: Yoke *(noun)* — the wooden frame used to join two oxen so they can pull the plow.

ZEALOT (ZELL-ut) *noun* — **someone with an extreme enthusiasm for a particular belief or activity; a fanatic**

Sounds like: sell it

Picture: A used-car salesman who is driven to sell as many cars as he can. His motto is "Sell it!" His zealous behavior is both admired and criticized by his co-workers. One day his zeal is curbed, at least momentarily, by one of his fellow salesmen, who rushes over to him and says, "What do you mean, 'Sell it'? That's <u>my</u> car!"

Other forms: Zeal, zealotry, zealousness *(nouns);* zealous *(adj);* zealously *(adv)*

ZENITH (ZEE-nith) *noun* — **the highest point; apex**

Sounds exactly like: Zenith (as in Zenith television sets)

Picture: King Kong climbing the Empire State Building (see APEX). When he gets to the top, he throws away the X, replacing it with a Zenith television. The TV is now at the highest point.

Other form: Zenithal *(adj)*

135 more

Here are another 135 words that I might have included in the main part of the book, but didn't. There were three possible reasons for excluding these words. (1) I may have thought enough people would already know the word. (2) I couldn't come up with an appropriate picture for the word. (3) I ran out of room. Whatever the reasons, these words are important for you to know. Some of them may very well appear on your SAT.

Admonish *(verb)* — to warn or scold, but in a caring way
Adversary *(noun)* — opponent; enemy
Aesthetic *(adj)* — appealing to the senses; beautiful
Animosity *(noun)* — a feeling of resentment, hostility, or enmity
Apprehension *(noun)* — nervousness; fear
Authoritarian *(adj)* — having complete control over many people
Autonomous *(adj)* — having the freedom of self-government; free
Blasphemy *(noun)* — disrespect toward God or something sacred
Blithe *(adj)* — merry; carefree
Comprehensive *(adj)* — covering completely; having broad scope
Conciliatory *(adj)* — agreeable; friendly; appeasing
Debilitate *(verb)* — to weaken
Delineate *(verb)* — to explain or describe in detail
Depravity *(noun)* — corruption; perversion; evil
Detached *(adj)* — separate; indifferent; aloof
Deterrent *(noun)* — something that prevents or discourages an act
Devious *(adj)* — tricky; crooked
Didactic *(adj)* — intended to teach; informative; instructional
Diligence *(noun)* — hard work; perseverance
Diminution *(noun)* — the act of decreasing
Discriminating *(adj)* — selecting carefully; judicious
Disinclination *(noun)* — tending to avoid; aversion
Dispassionate *(adj)* — not emotionally involved; objective
Disputatious *(adj)* — tending to argue; or, controversial
Disseminate *(verb)* — to spread or give out; to disburse
Dissonance *(noun)* — clashing sounds; lack of agreement
Document *(verb)* — to provide evidence; to back up with facts
Dubious *(adj)* — doubtful; questionable
Duplicity *(noun)* — sneakiness; contradiction; deceit
Elaborate *(verb)* — expand an explanation to include more details
Elusive *(adj)* — hard to catch or understand; evasive
Emaciated *(adj)* — extremely thin; wasted away
Embryonic *(adj)* — at an early stage of development
Engender *(verb)* — cause to exist; produce

Epic *(adj)* — large in scope or size

Equanimity *(noun)* — calmness; composure

Equivocal *(adj)* — misleading; uncertain

Erroneous *(adj)* — in error; false; mistaken

Execute *(verb)* — do what is requested; carry out

Exemplary *(adj)* — deserving imitation; serving as an example

Exemplify *(verb)* — show by example

Exhaustive *(adj)* — complete; thorough

Exonerate *(verb)* — to free from blame; to exculpate

Expedient *(adj)* — useful for reaching a desired end

Explicit *(adj)* — absolutely clear; free from ambiguity

Facilitate (verb) — make easier

Fanaticism *(noun)* — excessive, irrational enthusiasm

Fluctuate *(verb)* — to go up and down or back and forth

Frivolity *(noun)* — silliness; lack of seriousness

Gesticulate *(verb)* — to gesture dramatically when speaking

Glib *(adj)* — smooth-talking; slick

Grandiose *(adj)* — large; grand; filled with splendor

Gratuitous *(adj)* — free of charge; or, uncalled for and unwarranted

Haughty *(adj)* — proud to the point of being arrogant

Hedonism *(noun)* — the belief that only pleasure is worth pursuing

Hypothetical *(adj)* — not necessarily real; based upon supposition

Implement *(verb)* — to put into effect; to carry out

Implication *(noun)* — necessary result of an action; connection

Implicit *(adj)* — understood without explanation; or, inherent

Impugn *(verb)* — to attack with words; to accuse of being false

Impunity *(noun)* — freedom from punishment or harm

Incidental *(adj)* — happening by chance or luck; accidental

Incisive *(adj)* — direct; clear-cut; right to the point

Inclusive *(adj)* — covering or including everything

Incontrovertible *(adj)* — cannot be questioned or doubted

Indefatigable *(adj)* — having endless energy; tireless

Indifferent *(adj)* — impartial; unbiased; apathetic

Indiscriminate *(adj)* — without careful consideration; haphazard

Indulgent *(adj)* — giving in; yielding; lenient

Inherent *(adj)* — having a certain quality by nature; intrinsic

Insidious *(adj)* — gradually harmful; seductive

Instigate *(verb)* — to cause to act; urge; incite

Insuperable *(adj)* — incapable of being dominated or defeated

Intangible *(adj)* — not capable of being touched or perceived

Integrity *(noun)* — solidness of construction or morality; honesty

Interlocutor *(noun)* — someone who participates in a conversation

Interminable *(adj)* — endless

Methodical *(adj)* — step-by-step; sequential; systematic

Modicum *(noun)* — a very small amount

Nascent *(adj)* — recently born or created

Nebulous *(adj)* — unclear; vague

Notoriety *(noun)* — fame, usually obtained by doing something bad

Objective *(adj)* — without prejudice or bias; impartial; fair

Oblivion *(noun)* — the state of being forgotten
Oblivious *(adj)* — unaware; forgetful
Obtrusive *(adj)* — sticking out; or, pushy
Omniscient *(adj)* — knowing everything
Opalescent *(adj)* — reflecting a rainbow of color; dazzling
Ostentatious *(adj)* — overdone to the point of showing off; gaudy
Parochial *(adj)* — having a narrow view; restricted; local
Pedantic *(adj)* — obsessed with the details of knowledge; book-smart
Perturbation *(noun)* — disturbance
Philanthropy *(noun)* — charitable work; generosity
Plethora *(noun)* — over-abundance; excess
Poignancy *(noun)* — something that touches the emotions deeply
Pragmatic *(adj)* — practical
Presumptuous *(adj)* — going too far; overstepping the limits
Prevarication *(noun)* — a lie; mendacity
Proliferation *(noun)* — fast growth
Prolific *(adj)* — productive; fertile
Provincial *(adj)* — limited or restricted; parochial
Quiescent *(adj)* — calm; inactive; latent
Quintessential *(adj)* — being the best or purest example of something
Quixotic *(adj)* — idealistic; impractical (from Don Quixote)
Rebuke *(verb)* — criticize; reprimand; reprove
Rectify *(verb)* — to fix; to correct
Refute *(verb)* — prove wrong by showing evidence; deny
Renounce *(verb)* — to reject past beliefs or actions; repudiate
Reprehensible *(adj)* — deserving of criticism; culpable
Rescind *(verb)* — take back; remove; void
Retract *(verb)* — withdraw; take back a previous statement; recant
Sagacity *(noun)* — wisdom; shrewdness
Satire *(noun)* — a sarcastically humorous depiction
Saturate *(verb)* — fully satisfy; fill to capacity; soak
Savory *(adj)* — pleasing, either to the senses or the mind
Sedulous *(adj)* — hard-working and careful of details; diligent
Spendthrift *(noun)* — someone who wastes money (who is prodigal)
Stalwart *(adj)* — strong; unwavering
Stanch *(verb)* — to stop the flow of (blood, for example)
Staunch *(adj)* — standing firm; solidly loyal
Steadfast *(adj)* — not movable; strong in belief; staunch
Strident *(adj)* — harsh sounding
Stupefy *(verb)* — to cause someone to be groggy or confused
Submissive *(adj)* — tame; subservient; obsequious
Surpass *(verb)* — to go beyond; exceed
Tedious *(adj)* — long and drawn-out; tiresome; boring
Vagary *(noun)* — an unpredictable result or action
Vehement *(adj)* — strongly expressed; powerful
Venerate *(verb)* — respect greatly; revere
Viable *(adj)* — capable of living or functioning
Virtuoso *(noun)* — a highly-skilled person
Vociferous *(adj)* — loud and insistent; vehement; obstreperous
Vulnerable *(adj)* — able to be hurt
Whimsical *(adj)* — unpredictable; capricious

Sorry, Jac!

SAT Verbal:
Avoiding the Traps

You need a new attitude

For most of your test-taking career, you have been given exams made up by teachers who were on your side. They had taught you the material, and wanted you to prove they did a good job of it. So they were pulling for you to do well.

This may come as a surprise to you, but the people who create and administer the SAT don't especially want you to do well. At least not on their test. The SAT is designed to identify those students who are most likely to succeed in college. So if everyone did well on the SAT, the test would be useless.

Given that shocking bit of news, you must now arm yourself with a weapon you may have never before taken into the test-taking arena. It's called: thinking.

Now don't go getting your feelings hurt, or having bad thoughts about me and members of my family. I know you've done a lot of thinking on tests, and probably also during some other activities. But I'm talking about real, look 'em over extra good, how-are-they-trying-to-rip-me-off-this-time? thinking. I'm talking about being smart when some very sneaky people are trying to make you look dumb. I'm talking about being *suspicious*.

I'm also talking about knowing your stuff. Excelling on the SAT involves two things: the right attitude and the right knowledge. Go in without either one and you're going to get devoured, number-2 pencil and all.

What does SAT stand for?

It stands for Saturday, because that's the day the test is given. I thought everyone knew that. (Actually, it stands for Scholastic Assessment Test, but I don't really know what that means so I thought I'd joke around a little.)

How do the SAT testmakers try to trap you on the verbal part?

Mostly with vocabulary. The verbal part of the SAT is testing your ability to understand words and ideas. The testmakers (and colleges) want to see how familiar you are with the language. It's really as simple as that. It's also as complicated as that, because unfortunately, the language we're talking about here is English.

The fact that English may be your native language is quite irrelevant. English is filled, brimming, overflowing with areas of confusion. But because you haven't had to deal with them all at once, they haven't really posed much of a problem. Until now.

As you are no doubt beginning to suspect, the creators of the SAT have combed the English language for every possible source of trouble. And they've skillfully incorporated them into the very essence of the test. Here are a few of the most common:

1. Words that look alike but have different, sometimes opposite, meanings
2. Words that share roots with other words, but mean different things
3. Words that have a common and a less-common meaning
4. Words that have different meanings depending on how they're used
5. Words you know, but don't know you know
6. Words you think you know, but really don't
7. Strange words you may never see again after the SAT

And on and on. Need some real-life examples? Try these:

1. Words that look alike but have different, sometimes opposite, meanings
The word *condemn* means to harshly criticize. The word *condone* means to approve of. See the problem there? People confuse these two words all the time. The friendly folks at SAT-land know that. Which is why they like to use pairs of words like condemn and condone. One of the words will be in the question, and the meaning of the other will appear in the answer. Watch out!

2. Words that share roots with other words, but mean different things
We have all heard about Latin and Greek roots in many English words, and we were taught to connect those words in our minds. Most often this is a helpful thing to do. But once in a while it can create confusion. For example, the word *indolent* means lazy. On the other hand, *redolent* means fragrant. And, if you have one more hand, *doleful* means sad. Since each seems to have the root *-dole*, you might think the words are related. But as you can see from the definitions, there is much opportunity for the SAT to trap you.

3. Words that have a common and a less-common meaning
As a noun, the word *check* has several familiar meanings. It has a familiar meaning as a verb -- to inspect. But it also means to block (a body check in hockey, for example). The word champion may bring to mind a Super Bowl or World Series winner. But as a verb, to champion means to support -- as in "He championed the cause of animal rights." Other examples include: air, temper, trigger, hamper, founder, splinter, document, and wax. All have common and less-common meanings. On the SAT, expect the uncommon.

4. Words that have different meanings depending on how they're used
Sometimes the English language can be mildly bewildering. Sometimes it can be absolutely exasperating. Take, for example, the word *sanction*. As a verb, it means to approve, or give consent. I sanction your actions when I like what you're doing. However, as a noun, the word means the opposite. If the United States doesn't like North Korea's actions, the U.S. might issue economic sanctions against that nation. So sanction as a noun can mean an expression of disapproval or even punishment. (Hey, it's your language.)

5. Words you know, but don't know you know

Once you've learned the word *opaque*, it becomes a familiar word. It has that letter "q" in the middle, and there just aren't that many words like that. So you know *opaque*, as an adjective. But on the SAT, you just might see *opaque* as a noun: *opacity*. The "q" is gone. Will you recognize it?

6. Words you think you know, but really don't

You sort of know what *casual* means. You may not be able to put it into a distinct definition, but you can figure out the answer to a question involving this word. The SAT likes to use the word *causal*. Different word, different meaning. Did you catch it? It's easy to miss, because we don't proofread every word we read. We recognize many words by how they look. Unfortunately for you, the words *casual* and *causal* look very much alike. And on the SAT, that can mean only one thing: confusion. Here are a couple more examples. What do you think *quiescent* means? How about *noisome*? Look them up -- you may be surprised.

7. Strange words you may never see again after the SAT

Do you know what *necromancy* means? It refers to an activity involving communication with the dead. You might not expect to see it on the SAT. I've seen it on quite a few. How about *coven*? It means a group of witches. *Dross*? The impurities in metal. *Palisade*? A row of stakes. These are not common words in adult language, so why would the SAT people want you to know them? The simple answer is, they're hoping you don't.

A final point

Please remember, for every example you see here, there are dozens more I've seen on SATs. You'll see them, too, if you do enough practice tests. Eventually you will learn to recognize each kind of trap, even if you haven't seen every example of it before. And then you will be that much closer to your goal, because you will have learned how the testmakers think -- and how you must think.

Is there any guarantee the words in this book will appear on your test? No, only that some of them will. The problem is, we don't know which ones. But every new word you learn improves your odds by some fraction of a percent. So absorb these words, and others, wherever you can. And use them. Because even if you don't see *paucity*, *penchant*, or *perfunctory* on the SAT, knowing them will enrich your life just a little bit.

I hope this book has done the same.

Don't be fooled!

Here's a sampling of the word pairs and groups employed by the SAT to confuse and confound your brain. This list is far from complete, but it will give you an idea of the kinds of words to watch out for.

These have different (sometimes opposite) meanings:

apprehend *and* apprehensive
comprehend *and* comprehensive
condone *and* condemn
ingenious *and* ingenuous
arid *and* arable
casual *and* causal
loath *and* loathe
collaborate *and* corroborate
parity *and* parody
indignant, indigenous, *and* indigent
prescribe *and* proscribe
disperse *and* disburse
dole, redolent, *and* indolent
censure *and* censor
chasten *and* chaste
pity *and* piety
erratic *and* erotic
decadent *and* decade
quiescent *and* quiet
noisome *and* noisy
disparage *and* disparate
prodigy, prodigal, *and* prodigious
timorous *and* temerity
enervate *and* energize
arcane *and* archaic
thrift *and* spendthrift
compliment *and* complement
wary *and* weary
persecute *and* prosecute
ambiguous *and* ambivalent
voluble *and* valuable
dissemble *and* disassemble
impudent *and* impotent
invidious *and* insidious
proceed *and* precede
conceited *and* conceded
dissent *and* descent
profound *and* profane
innate *and* inane

These mean a group of something:

coven (witches)
pride (lions)
phalanx (soldiers)
troupe (performers)

These mean talkative:	*These mean quiet:*
loquacious	laconic
garrulous	reticent
verbose	taciturn
voluble	terse

These mean scold or criticize:		*These mean praise:*
admonish	disparage	acclaim
castigate	rebuke	accolade
censure	reprove	extol
chasten	upbraid	laud
chastise		lionize

These are just weird words you have to know for the SAT:

dross (impurities)
slag (impurities)
charlatan (faker)
necromancy (communication with the dead)
sorcerer (someone who communicates with the dead)
conflagration (big fire)
palisade (row of stakes)

100 SAT MATH TIPS
AND HOW TO MASTER THEM NOW!

A FEW MORE HOURS OF THIS AND I'LL BE ABLE TO TAKE A WHOLE DAY OFF!

I LOVE MATH!

This book does more than just teach you how to solve the problem. It teaches you how to <u>see</u> the problem, how to recognize and avoid the traps, and how to think! Using SAT-style math questions to demonstrate 100 critical concepts, *100 SAT Math Tips* turns the scared student into a fearless giant killer. The ammunition: straight talk, solid information, humor, crystal-clear diagrams, cartoons, teaching boxes, a complete glossary, cross-referenced index, and 30 additional practice questions! *(120 pages, $14.95)*

If your local educational resource store doesn't have *100 SAT Math Tips*, ask them to order it today!

Mostly Bright Ideas
888-301-2829
http://www.mostlybrightideas.com

Burdick Associates
800-828-1434
716-335-8807 (fax)

CIRCUMFERENCE, RADIUS, DIAMETER, π

CAN YOU HELP ME WITH DIFFERENTIATION OF LOGARITHMIC FUNCTIONS?

SURE, BUT FIRST I HAVE TO MAKE A WEE-WEE